Trusting God Through Troubles & Tears

CINDY ROOY

WESTBOW®
PRESS
A DIVISION OF THOMAS NELSON
& ZONDERVAN

WestBow Press books may be ordered through booksellers or by contacting:

WestBow Press
A Division of Thomas Nelson & Zondervan
1663 Liberty Drive
Bloomington, IN 47403
www.westbowpress.com
1 (866) 928-1240

ISBN: 978-1-4908-9188-0 (sc)
ISBN: 978-1-4908-9189-7 (e)

Print information available on the last page.

WestBow Press rev. date: 10/03/2017

Contents

Acknowledgments v

A Note From The Author vi

Helpful Hints to Leading a Bible Study Group viii

Introduction Session (Optional) ix

Chapter One: Do You Trust God? 1
    Day One: My Ability to Trust 1
    Day Two: God's Trustworthiness 4
    Day Three: Bible Belief 7
    Day Four: Opposition 10
    Day Five: Knowing God 13
    Chapter One Discussion/Review Questions 17

Chapter Two: God's Power 19
    Day One: Universe 19
    Day Two: Nature 22
    Day Three: Creatures 25
    Day Four: People 27
    Day Five: Nations/Government Leaders 30
    Chapter Two Discussion/Review Questions 34

Chapter Three: God's Knowledge 36
    Day One: God Knows Us Best 36
    Day Two: Knowledge and Understanding 39
    Day Three: Spiritual Wisdom 42
    Day Four: Wisdom's Benefits 45
    Day Five: Be Wise 48
    Chapter Three Discussion/Review Questions 52

Chapter Four: God's Love 54
    Day One: Biblical Descriptions and Assurances 54
    Day Two: Biblical Evidences of God's Love 57
    Day Three: Personalize God's Love 61
    Day Four: Our Response 64
    Day Five: Second Chances 68
    Chapter Four Discussion/Review Questions 72

Chapter Five: Troubles and Tears   **74**

    Day One: Biblical Troubles   74

    Day Two: Today's Troubles   77

    Day Three: Reasons For Troubles   80

    Day Four: Reasons For Troubles Part 2   84

    Day Five: Reasons For Troubles Part 3   89

    Chapter Five Discussion/Review Questions   94

Chapter Six: Choosing To Trust God   **96**

    Day One: Will Over Feelings   96

    Day Two: Excuses   99

    Day Three: When God Is Silent   102

    Day Four: Why Pray?   106

    Day Five: Benefits of Trusting God   109

    Chapter Six Discussion/Review Questions   114

Endnotes   **116**

Personal Notes   **117**

Acknowledgments

God orchestrated this book project and used several people to convince, encourage, and assist me. After participating in a Bible study that I wrote and led at a church retreat, Dianne Barker introduced the idea of getting published and attending a Christian Writers Conference. Her persistence and persuasiveness resulted in my praying about it. Consequently, I received overwhelming confirmation from God with opened doors to proceed. Thank you, Dianne, for what you claimed—listening to and obeying God in prodding me to take action.

Donna Hanegraaff is my life's sounding board and prayer warrior. Her enthusiastic approval of this endeavor surprised and motivated me. She also took the front cover picture of the sunset over Lake Michigan. Thanks, Donna! Our lifelong friendship is a blessing to me.

I appreciate Steve and Carole Lyons who provided affirmation and proofread the text for biblical accuracy, and Kathy Anderson for editing the grammar.

Melanie Rutstrom provided helpful editing as she individually worked through the study. Melanie, your support encouraged me and I'm grateful for all the time you've put into this workbook and selflessly assisted me. Thank you, my friend.

Karen Boatright and Cathy Leming organized and led a group of ladies in a test run of this Bible study, and gave valuable feedback. Thanks, Karen, for opening your home, and Cathy, for believing in me from day one. I treasure your friendships! I appreciate the Bible study members for giving their time and comments.

Jim, I needed your total support and you gave it. Besides buying a computer and desk for me, you didn't complain about a lack of income. All the times I wrote instead of cleaned the house, you were silent. Thank you, my husband, for your Christian faith and willingness to partner with me in this venture.

Most importantly, my heavenly Father spoke to my heart, presented affirming confirmation every time I doubted, provided for my needs before I had to ask, and gave me the energy and strength to write for hours on end. It was incredible how fast the time passed when I was in the Word. Thank You, Father, for allowing me to see Your hand in every aspect of this project, and for giving me such joy in composing this study. Your faithfulness to me was noticeable.

It was amazing how the Holy Spirit gave me ideas and the words to write. Thank You, Spirit, for equipping me for the task You set before me. I am so thankful for the undeniable divine help I received while writing.

Now Lord, I ask that You bless everyone who works through this Bible study. May You speak to them and act in their lives like You have in mine. And in the end, may You be forever praised and glorified by all, Amen.

A Note From The Author

Hello my friends! Welcome to this topical Bible study about trusting God. This workbook has six chapters, each consisting of five lessons and chapter review questions that foster group discussion. Before you start, allow me to introduce myself and share my motivation in writing *Trusting God Through Troubles & Tears*.

I am one of those people who just cannot remember when I accepted the Lord as my Savior. I started attending church in my mother's womb. My father thought it was important for me to spend my formative years in Christian schools, so all of my education – elementary, high school, and college – took place in Christian institutions. I made my profession of faith formally in a church when I was 16, but I had a relationship with God long before that. I remember privately praying to God in first grade.

Nevertheless, I didn't realize my deep personal need for the Lord until I got married after my junior year of college. Dealing with a volatile marriage, being a full-time student, and paying monthly bills opened my eyes to life being difficult. I learned to wear a fake smile while I struggled on the inside. I had all of this biblical knowledge but did not understand how to apply it to myself. It stayed in my head but didn't enter my heart. I tried to deal with my problems without God because I reasoned that if He allowed me to have them, He wasn't going to take them away. When that self-reliant method failed, I started praying for help. But I didn't want God to help me persevere through my troubles; no, I begged Him to make them disappear. God allowed that attitude to go on for years before He finally intervened.

While secretly suffering, I saw life-threatening and painful adversities that some of my relatives were going through. And I realized that life is not fair for anyone. While God dealt with me - educating and healing me spiritually through years of Bible studies - my siblings were not getting relief from their hardships. One underwent 17 surgeries and another suffered an auto-immune breakdown - losing his health, job, and family. I could not understand why God, if He supposedly loved us, allowed so many disappointments, heartaches, and constant pain. I questioned if He was really in control. So I searched the Scriptures to find some answers. What I learned surprised me.

All people experience troubles and tears, some more often than others. By sharing my stories and the discoveries of my study, perhaps others can prevent wasting years of their lives misunderstanding God and living their lives without peace and joy.

Writing a book was never a desire of mine, but God had a plan and provided repeated confirmation concerning the call to write this Bible study. I responded with lots of prayer for guidance.

As you work through this book, it will be easier (but not required) if you use the 1984 New International Version Bible to answer the questions. The references given are from that version, unless specifically noted. If you do not have a 1984 NIV Bible, you can gain access to it through the internet and download a free app.

Being a former student and teacher, I like variety in the homework. So you will find a mix of matching, fill-in-the-blanks, check or circle all that applies, short answers, and thought or application questions. At the end of each chapter are discussion and review questions for group studies. There is an average of 3 discussion/review questions per lesson and they can be answered immediately after your day's lesson or left for a sixth day of study. Whether you are doing this Bible study by yourself or as a group, I encourage you to actually write out your answers to all the questions. Some questions may take more thought than others, but working through them brings better retention and growth in your spiritual life.

If you are in a group study, don't hold back in sharing your answers. You may think your answer isn't very good, but more times than not, it is just what another person needs to hear. You can learn as much from the discussion as you can working through the lessons.

Begin each lesson by asking the Holy Spirit to help you absorb whatever information He deems beneficial for you that day, and to give you insight as you read the material and answer the questions. With His help, every minute invested will be worthwhile.

Finally, my prayer is that your mind will be attentive to your heavenly Father speaking to you through this Bible study. I pray that you will be greatly encouraged in your spiritual walk with God and motivated to trust Him through every adverse situation you experience. And somewhere in these pages, may our Lord Jesus Christ touch you and leave His fingerprint on your heart.

Helpful Hints to Leading a Bible Study Group

If you have never led a Bible study before, the following suggestions may help.

~ One hour of time is needed for this group study. If an additional 15 minutes is available, that is even better. The extra time will allow a full hour for discussion plus prayer requests and updates to be shared before the closing prayer. Begin and end each session with prayer.

~ Arrange the seats in a circle (if possible). Discussion is easier when everyone can see each other's face. If you serve coffee and/or snacks, provide a table to sit around. It's a bit awkward to handle food, drink, Bible, workbook, and pen at the same time.

~ If your group is larger than 15, consider breaking up into two or more discussion groups. This allows more people to answer questions and participate in the discussion.

~ Take time to pray before the group convenes. Ask the Lord to help you facilitate the discussion and for His blessing upon all who attend.

~ Smile and relax. Just be yourself and allow others to see your weaknesses. They will feel more comfortable around you and be more willing to share their answers.

~ The group will become more talkative as they get to know each other. If there is a question that no one wants to answer first, you (as the leader) share your answer. Then ask to hear how they responded to that question. Remind the group that many of the questions have no right or wrong answers. We learn from each other by sharing our thoughts, experiences, and faith.

~ Do not let one person dominate the discussion. If this happens, immediately after reading the next question, ask to hear from those who haven't contributed yet.

~ Be aware of the time, (wear a watch if there isn't a clock in the room), and move the discussion along so that every question is addressed. Some participants may be waiting to hear the answers to the last question. Divide the number of questions by the time allotted and you have an idea for the average amount of time per question. As a courtesy to every person present, do your best to start and end on time.

Introduction Session (Optional)

Decide whether your Bible study group needs an additional introduction class. Benefits from choosing to meet an extra day include having the opportunity to distribute the books, and to get to know one another in the group. The following suggestions are to help the leader introduce the study and set the tone for the following weeks:

As you welcome each person, give them a name tag to fill out and wear (if there is a chance that any person in the group does not know another's name). Bring extra pens in case someone forgets one or their ink runs out.

Open the session with prayer.

Ask the participants to introduce themselves with general information (family, job, hobbies) and answer the question, "What is your favorite food?" The leader shares first, then go around the circle. This should take up most of the time. Providing an opportunity for the group members to learn about each other enables them to bond sooner.

Promote faith in the environment; comment on the significance of everyone keeping the conversation of this group confidential. No one will share their answers if they think others will gossip about them. Make sure everyone is in agreement.

Emphasize the advantage of using the 1984 New International Version Bible to answer the fill-in-the-blanks. Perhaps someone will have an extra NIV Bible in their house to lend out if another person does not possess one. The 1984 NIV Bible can also be accessed through the internet and by downloading a free app on your mobile device.

Recommend reading *A Note From the Author*. This will help them get acquainted with the author and learn why this Bible study was written. Additional tips are given to help the reader have a successful experience in completing the workbook.

Stress the value of completing each lesson and the discussion/review questions at the end of each chapter. Although one can contribute without answering these questions, discussion will be enhanced when the participants put some previous thought into their answers.

Encourage the participants to journal. Three lines are provided after every lesson for writing a personal prayer, question, or one's thoughts. Ask if anyone currently journals. Perhaps one or two people will share the blessings they've experienced from recording their prayers and insights.

Point out that there are some empty pages with the title *Personal Notes* in the back of the workbook. These pages are for recording thoughts and memories that come to mind while completing the study, and for note taking or extra journaling. Any good answers or comments made by others during discussion time can be written down on these pages. The space may also be used to record the prayer requests of the group.

After delivering this information, ask for prayer requests and then close the session in prayer.

Chapter One: Do You Trust God?

Day One: My Ability to Trust

How easy is it for you to trust other people? Have you ever been taken advantage of, scammed, or betrayed? Has a close friend ever revealed a secret of yours to another person? Which of these people do you trust? Circle all that apply.

spouse	friend	neighbor	brother/sister	waiter/waitress
doctor	pastor	hitchhiker	children	car mechanic
coach	parent	babysitter	local police	boss/employees
realtor	teacher	hair stylist	politician	used-car salesman

On the lines below, write the names of anyone you trust who were not included in the list above.

_____

_____

Why do you trust these people? What characteristics do they possess that allow you to trust them?

_____

_____

Can you trust God? Do you believe that He is present when disasters occur? Does He care what happens to you? Do you believe that God is active on your behalf? Rate the amount of trust you think you have in God, with the number 0 representing none and 10 total trust.

None--Total

    0   1   2   3   4   5   6   7   8   9   10

Sometimes we don't want to trust God, but try to fix the problem ourselves. When dealing with a crisis, we don't intentionally leave God out, we just forget to include Him. We react to the problem first, then think about it, maybe act again, and then finally pray when we realize we didn't help the situation at all. We turn to God as a last resort.

So often when I encounter problems, I ask God for help and then tell Him how I want Him to help me. Sometimes, I react without consulting Him at all. And occasionally, I give the problem to the Lord and get impatient if He doesn't work fast enough for me. Then I take the problem back and try to make things happen on my own. But I end up with a mess from trying to fix the situation myself. As a result, the problem becomes more complicated and even appears to be out of control. However, it's only out of my control. I must trust God to do it His way and on His timetable.

Do you have any personal issues you don't trust God with, but instead have your mind set on your own agenda? In what areas of your life do you have a hard time giving Him total control?

_____

_____

_____

Be honest with yourself and identify why you have difficulty giving up control in those areas. What do you fear or what do you hope to accomplish?

_____

_____

Let's take a closer look at the word "trust." What does that word mean to you?

_____

_____

Throughout the Bible, instructions are given to trust God; do you? Do you believe everything written in the Bible is accurate? _____ Do you believe in its truth with enough conviction to act upon its principles? _____ Are you reluctant to trust God, afraid that He will disappoint you? Read Psalm 22:4-5. What are the three results David's ancestors experienced from trusting God?

_____

_____

_____

> "As the Scripture says, 'Anyone who trusts in him will never be put to shame.'"
> Romans 10:11

Have you ever been ridiculed by others for your faith? Do you fear being rejected or targeted because you actively trust in God? _____ Take a look (in the inset of this page) at Romans 10:11. What does this verse say about the person who trusts in God?

_____

_____

In this verse, the word "trust" is the translation of *pisteuo*, a Greek verb meaning "to commit to, to have faith, with an implication to entrust one's spiritual well-being to Christ."[1] What about the times when God doesn't give us what we want? Or when He allows some trouble or heartache in our lives? How are we to trust God when it doesn't seem like He is working on our behalf? Look up Proverbs 3:5. Write your answer below.

_____

_____

_____

> *Our ability to trust God wholeheartedly depends on our belief in who He is.*

In biblical terms, the heart is not only the home of one's emotions and affections, but also of the intellect and will.[2] We are to trust God with all of our heart (whole-hearted vs. half-hearted). This conscious and willful act acknowledges that God is aware of our situation and is in control.

Furthermore, in order to trust God without hesitation, there has to be a relationship with Him. Normally, we do not trust strangers because we don't know them. Well, it is the same with the Lord; if we do not know Him personally, we probably won't fully trust Him.

God wants us to have confidence in Him and to rely on Him. We are told more than one hundred times in Scripture to trust in the Lord our God. And to be able to trust Him completely, we need to know Him intimately. Our ability to trust God wholeheartedly depends on our belief in His identity. Who is God to you?

_____

_____

_____

Knowing God entails more than just knowing about God. When we know God, we have a deep personal relationship with Him as a result of seeking Him and experiencing Him. In the Bible, God reveals a great deal about Himself and encourages us to experience Him – to put our belief into action and taste His goodness and power. And when we exercise our faith, God discloses even more of Himself to us, which increases our desire to know and experience Him further. Read Psalm 9:10 and fill in the blanks.

"Those who _____ your name will _____ in

_____, for you, Lord, have _____ forsaken those who

_____ you."

In the Hebrew text, the word "trust" is a strong verb referring to confidence and being sure.[3] It is more than belief; it is an unbending conviction that God will not fail. David is saying that to know God is to trust Him. When we seek Him, we will find Him and He will never leave us no matter what we face. In Psalm 34:8 we read, "Taste and see that the Lord is good" and in Psalm 145:9, "The Lord is good to all." We may have our doubts about trusting others, but we have no reason to fear trusting God.

As we work through this Bible study, we will examine who God is, His character, reasons for our troubles, and why we should trust Him. Every lesson ends with two suggestions to be included in your prayer. Lines are provided to write anything else you would like to include, or perhaps jot down a question or mention whatever touched your heart that day. Journaling has many benefits—both immediate and later on—so give it a try.

Prayer For Today:

Thank God for wanting a personal relationship with you and for His encouragement to trust Him.

Ask God to help you know Him better, experience Him more, and learn to trust Him with all of your heart, starting in the areas where you are hesitant.

_____

_____

_____

If the Lord is your co-pilot, change seats!

Day Two: God's Trustworthiness

> "Do not let your hearts be troubled. Trust in God; trust also in me."
> John 14:1

When my youngest child received his driver's license and became independent, I wanted to get a job outside of the house. Since I was feeling my age and my resume lacked any work experience for ten years, I no longer felt qualified to do much of anything. I wanted a part-time job, possibly in the medical field, but I knew I needed God's help to find something that I could physically do and enjoy. So I prayed that God would choose my employer and cause that person to call and offer me a job. I wasn't being lazy, but trusted Him to help me, because after two months of searching, I was finding closed doors. I based my hopes and trust on Jeremiah 29:11 - a verse in which God says He has plans for you. In less than three weeks, I received a phone call from a local dentist who was expanding her office; she told me I had been recommended to her for the new position. God actually gave me a part-time medical job that I loved!

Have you found God to be trustworthy? He may give us the desires of our hearts, but is He dependable in times of trouble? Read John 14:1 in the inset. Who is speaking? _____
What were Jesus' instructions? _____

When our hearts are troubled, we tend to worry. Worry causes stress in our bodies, and stress can cause all sorts of ailments. To worry is to not trust God.

I became anxious over my children when they were teenagers and drove their cars. Every time I heard a siren, I wanted to grab my cell phone and call them to make sure they were okay. It took me a long time to be able to relax and not panic when I heard tires screech in the distance or sirens blaring.

Jesus instructed His disciples (and us) not to worry. Read Matthew 6:25-34 and leave a bookmark there. Then read Luke 12:22-31 and compare the two texts.

1. According to Matthew 6:26 and Luke 12:24, what did Jesus say?

_____

_____

2. From Matthew 6:30 and Luke 12:28, what did Jesus reveal about our faith?

_____

_____

3. What comfort do you find in Matthew 6:32 and Luke 12:30?

_____

_____

> "Therefore do not worry about tomorrow for tomorrow will worry about itself. Each day has enough trouble of its own."
> Matthew 6:34

We learn from these verses that our Father in heaven knows all of our needs, and because we are valuable to Him, He will provide for us. When we worry, we display little faith in Him. If you compare the passages, Matthew has one verse that Luke doesn't record. Read Matthew 6:34 in the inset. Jesus was speaking and He concluded the section with "therefore," meaning "considering all that I have just said, now apply this." He continued with, "do not worry about tomorrow…" Jesus wants us to trust God and not worry, for our Father will take care of our needs and troubles. As our Father in heaven daily feeds the birds of the air, He values us much more and will also provide for us!

I should have trusted my Father in heaven more with the safety of my teenaged drivers and not have worried so much. (Worrying is a lot like being in a rocking chair. There is a lot of activity, but it gets you nowhere.) Do you have faith that God will take care of you? Do you believe He will watch over your family or other loved ones? Let's look at three of God's attributes that make Him so trustworthy. Fill in the blanks.

1. God has _____. Romans 11:33a

2. God has great _____. Psalm 103:11

3. The Lord is _____ and comes with _____. Isaiah 40:10a

God has unlimited knowledge and wisdom. He knows what is best for us and what we need. God's love has no limit and He wants what is best for each of us. God is sovereign (supreme in power and authority); He has complete control and rules over everything. His power is unmatched and He is able to do what is best for us. If God loves us and wants the best for us, has infinite wisdom and knows what is best for us, and has the power and authority to cause it to happen, can we trust Him with our lives? You bet. What did David say about God in 2 Samuel 7:28?

_____

_____

> *God loves us and wants the best for us, has infinite wisdom and knows what is best for us, and has the power and authority to cause it to happen.*

David claimed that God is sovereign and in control. He declared God's words to be trustworthy, and that He's the giver of good things. Read Psalm 111:7 and 119:138. How do these verses compare?

_____

_____

The same adjective "trustworthy" is used. God's words and His statutes (laws) and precepts (rules of conduct or moral instructions) are totally dependable. Everything about God is trustworthy. If we acknowledge this truth, why do we have such a difficult time trusting Him?

_____

_____

One answer may be our depravity – our inborn nature to sin. We might have no problem giving God control over certain areas of our lives, but our sinful pleasures are always the hardest to give up. Yet, God promises it will be worth it; we just need to try trusting Him and see for ourselves. "…Blessed is he who trusts in the Lord" (Proverbs 16:20). And in Jeremiah 17:7 we read, "Blessed is the man who trusts in the Lord, whose confidence is in him." Are you experiencing God's blessings? One of these blessings is living without worry.

Prayer For Today:

Thank God that He is completely trustworthy.

Ask God to help you trust Him for every situation that causes you to worry.

_____

_____

_____

Day Three: Bible Belief

Do you know of people who pick and choose what they believe inside the Bible? They select and accept whatever verse they think supports their claim, but conveniently ignore or disbelieve those verses which support an opposing view or convict them. We know that the Bible is either completely true – the words contained in it are trustworthy – or it is not true and the book is unreliable.

The Bible's authors were equipped by the Holy Spirit (2 Peter 1:20-21), and they wrote in compliance with God's divine will. Paul affirmed God's involvement in the writing of Scripture (2 Timothy 3:16), and called it the infallible and authoritative Word of God. According to Proverbs 30:5, "Every word of God is flawless…" Read Psalm 18:30 and 2 Samuel 22:31. How do these two passages, written by different people, compare to Proverbs 30:5?

_____

_____

God's faithfulness to His words and promises are mentioned repeatedly in both the Old and New Testament. Several different authors who knew the Lord testified to this same truth.

What did Moses emphasize in Deuteronomy 7:9?

_____

_____

What did Paul proclaim in 1 Corinthians 1:9?

_____

_____

Read Psalm 145:13b in the inset. David wrote frequently about the Lord's faithfulness in Psalms. He claimed that God's promises have been thoroughly tested and that he loved them (Psalm 119:140). Joshua testified that every good promise God gave has come true and been fulfilled; not one has failed (Joshua 23:14-15). And Paul confirmed this in 2 Corinthians 1:20 declaring, "For no matter how many promises God has made, they are 'Yes' in Christ." Each of these men in different times of history believed and experienced that God is true to His word and keeps every promise.

> "The Lord is faithful to all his promises and loving toward all he has made."
> Psalm 145:13b

Fill in the blanks to complete Psalm 119:160.

" _____ your _____ are _____; _____

your _____ _____ are _____."

David found comfort in God's words because 1) they are true and 2) they are not fickle but are grounded firmly in the Lord's unchanging moral character. God's words are accurate and relevant forever!

The Bible's amazing accuracy has stood the bibliographical test with over 24,000 manuscripts in Greek and Latin. The internal test shows that many flawed people wrote it with no contradictions. The Bible's external test reveals its accuracy with many archeological finds and all the ancient reliable documents separate from the manuscript. These three tests—bibliographical, internal, and external—support the historical authenticity of the Bible.

> "Fix these words of mine in your hearts and minds…teach them to your children, talking about them when you sit at home and when you walk along the road, when you lie down and when you get up."
> Deuteronomy 11:18-19

There are other factors which support the Bible's uniqueness. The Bible is the only one of its kind; it's a composition of 66 books that covered over a 1,500 year span with 40 different authors that has consistency throughout. Its existence is due to divine intervention. (No wonder it is called "God's Word.")

Furthermore, the Bible's durability is remarkable. Recorded in Matthew 24:35, Jesus prophesied that "heaven and earth will pass away but my words will never pass away." The Bible has survived and thrived for over 2,000 years. It is the most distributed book of all times and the most attacked. It was hand copied and yet endured. Peter called it "the living and enduring word of God" (1Peter 1:23). In Isaiah 40:8, we read that the Word of God stands forever.

If there was no truth to what God said, the Bible would not exist. Yet, David, Joshua, Paul, and others experienced these truths for themselves and had to testify about them. They all declared that God's Word contains nothing useless or worthless, but is totally trustworthy.

Have you discovered for yourself that the words in the Bible are still valid and true? Have you personally experienced biblical truths? _____ If your answer is yes, what were they?

_____

_____

God wants us to not only read and believe His words, but to act on them. James advised us, "Do not merely listen to the word, and so deceive yourselves. Do what it says" (James 1:22). From Deuteronomy 11:18-19, what did God tell us to do with His words? (The passage is in the inset.)

_____

_____

_____

How do we fix God's words in our hearts and minds? _____
We read His words, then study, discuss, and memorize them. We teach them to others. Read
the analogy Jesus gave, recorded in Luke 6:46-49. What did the Lord compare with putting His
words into practice?

_____

_____

How did the author of Hebrews 4:12 describe the words of God?

_____

_____

_____

God's Word is a living power that judges with an eye that sees everything and can penetrate
a person's innermost being. God knows every thought, attitude, motive, and heart, and reaches
out to them. When studying His Word, have you ever felt that inner conviction—like a piercing
of your soul—and sensed the passage was speaking directly to you? That is God's Word being
active and working in you. It is always effective. The Lord said:

> As the rain and the snow come down from heaven, and do not return to
> it without watering the earth and making it bud and flourish...so is my
> word that goes out from my mouth: It will not return to me empty, but
> will accomplish what I desire and achieve the purpose for which I sent it.
> (Isaiah 55:10-11)

*The best method
of learning
about God's
trustworthiness is
to experience God
rather than just
read about Him.*

One difference between belief in the Bible and unbelief is
experience. Anyone who tests God's words will personally realize
that the Bible is true and God is faithful to all His promises.
The best method of learning about God's trustworthiness is to
experience God rather than just read about Him.

My husband and I are convinced that the words of the Bible
are true and it was proven to us in the field of tithing. According
to Malachi 3, God challenged His people to test Him in tithes
and offerings. The opportunity presented itself and we took His
challenge. When I was pregnant with our first child, I quit my job
and we lost one-half of our income. We were tempted to give less
money to the church because we knew there might not be enough to pay our bills. But with faith,
my husband gave the usual 10%. We had been as frugal as possible and prayed that God would
take care of our needs. Soon afterwards, we received a phone call notifying us that our insurance
agent left the company and a new representative would visit us that week. We discovered that
our old agent never updated our information and our car premium was erroneous - we had been
overpaying for a couple of years. Consequently, we were given the option of receiving credit or a
check. That check covered more than what we needed.

There were other monetary incidents which provided another unexpected check and even a desired television. We cannot out-give God! God shows His believers how great He is by being faithful to His words.

Have you tested the Bible's trustworthiness? When has God's Word entered your heart and caused a response from you? _____
Have you ever experienced God's power and faithfulness in your life or witnessed it in someone else's? _____ If yes, did it change you? Have you shared your story with others?

Once we realize that the Bible is truth and it has power to transform lives, our ability to trust God increases. Wise men teach God's "true and reliable words" so that our "trust may be in the Lord" (Proverbs 22:19-21).

Prayer For Today:

Thank God for the accessibility of the Bible in America and the freedom we have to read, study, and learn from it.

Ask God to lead you to the Bible passages that will validate your belief, speak to you personally, and encourage you to trust Him.

_____

_____

_____

Day Four: Opposition

Satan would like nothing better than to turn believers away from the Lord. He is the author and master of obstacles to our faith and trust. He is also known as "that ancient serpent",[4] "the devil",[5] the "accuser",[6] and "Beelzebub".[7] Satan is an angel who rebelled against God and was thrown out of heaven (Luke 10:18). As a created being, Satan has limitations. He tempts us because he would like us to reject God and live his kind of life.

Satan tempted Eve and succeeded in getting her to want to be like God and consequently disobey Him. Satan even tempted Jesus, but Jesus resisted him and did not sin. Being tempted is not a sin; succumbing to temptation is. Read James 1:12. What are the blessings and rewards for those who don't give in when tempted, but trust God during their trials?

_____

_____

Satan roams throughout the earth and goes back and forth in it;[8] he stirs up trouble for God's followers. Although God permits Satan to work in our world, God is still in control and

Satan is under God's rule. Satan's plans never outsmart God; on the contrary, God uses Satan to accomplish His purposes.

The more you trust and serve the Lord God, the more opposition from Satan you will likely encounter. His plan is to use:

> "You, dear children, are from God and have overcome them, because the one who is in you is greater than the one who is in the world."
> 1 John 4:4

- Doubt, which makes you question God's word and His goodness

- Discouragement, which causes you to look at the problems and focus on the obstacles rather than on God

- Diversion, which makes the wrong things seem attractive so you will want them

- Defeat, which makes you feel like a failure so you won't even try

- Delay, which makes you put off doing something so it never gets done[9]

We must remember that God is greater than Satan and through prayer, Satan is overcome. Read 1 John 4:4 in the inset. What does this verse mean to you?

_____

_____

Why don't we have to fear Satan? First of all, followers of Jesus Christ are God's children. Secondly, God is greater than Satan. Another definitive answer is found in 2 Thessalonians 3:3. Fill in the blanks.

"But the Lord is _____, and he will

_____ and _____ you from

_____ _____ _____."

Every type of opposition that Satan uses can cause one to become disheartened. However, there is nothing better to boost your faith in God than to see first-hand that God the Father, Son, and Holy Spirit are more powerful and sovereign over Satan. Witnessing Satan being evicted from a person, (who was a highest level Satanist), by speaking God's words as recorded in the Bible, is an unforgettable experience. I am amazed how the Word of God is alive and active and so powerful.

> *The Lord is faithful, and He will strengthen and protect you from the evil one.*

Of course, Jesus exemplified this when Satan tempted Him.[10] Jesus taught us how to respond to Satan, and that is by quoting Scripture. Scripture is a piece of the armor of God, discussed in Ephesians 6:11-17.

Read verse 17 in the inset. What is the sword of the Spirit?_____

Speaking God's words or quoting Scripture triumphs over Satan. God's Word rules! If you read the entire Ephesian passage listed above, notice that the sword (word of God) is the only weapon of offense in that list of armor. Perhaps it is so effective that no other is needed.

> "Take the helmet of salvation and the sword of the Spirit, which is the word of God."
> Ephesians 6:17

Other forms of opposition can also keep us from trusting God. Society has gradually become intolerant to Christianity and the Bible. The American government has interpreted law in such a way that the Bible is no longer allowed to be taught in public school classrooms and public prayer has been banned. Judges are interpreting laws to reflect their own values, and immoral laws have been created which are in direct violation of God's commands. Furthermore, our own human depravity or tendency to sin causes us to to love the world, question our faith, and put our trust in other things besides God.

We have plenty of obstacles that hinder us from trusting God; Satan uses every trick to keep God's children from something spiritually beneficial (like attending Bible studies). Trusting in a divine being may seem futile to unbelievers, but they haven't had the privilege of experiencing the Lord's faithfulness and goodness.

What kinds of opposition seem to be most effective in your life to keep you from trusting God?

_____

_____

_____

Perhaps by identifying these oppositions, you can better recognize them when they attack you. Then you can ask God for help in persevering through those difficult times - to remain faithful, to stay in His Word, and to trust Him.

It's reassuring to read so many passages in the Bible that strengthen and encourage us to trust God when we face opposition. Our Lord will give us a verse that is just what we need to focus on when we are weak. Read Nahum 1:7 in the inset. What does the Lord do for those who trust in Him?

> "The Lord is good, a refuge in times of trouble. He cares for those who trust in him."
> Nahum 1:7

_____

_____

Thank God that He is sovereign over Satan and that you have God's words to overcome any opposition you encounter.

Ask God to encourage, strengthen, and protect you if you are currently facing opposition, and to boost your resolve to continue to trust in Him.

_____

_____

_____

Day Five: Knowing God

What is meant by the word "know?" The NIV Bible dictionary defines it as, "to discern, recognize, acknowledge, learn, or to be intimately familiar with." How well we know God is related to how much we trust Him. The more we learn about God, the more confident we are in trusting Him.

> *How much we trust God is related to how well we know Him.*

The story of Enoch is short but fascinating. He walked and talked with God for 300 years and one day God took him — Enoch did not experience death (Genesis 5:22-24; Hebrews 11:5). Can you imagine how well we could get to know God if we had 300 years? We don't need that much time because now we have the Bible in which God reveals Himself to us. But do we read it? Do we comprehend what we read?

"Be still and know that I am God" (Psalm 46:10). Being still means silence on the outside and surrender on the inside. Every day we need to take a few moments and be still, and listen to God. The Lord imparts knowledge to us when we make time for Him – time to read His words in the Bible and meditate on them, and time to listen for Him to speak to us. God our Father emphatically said to listen to Jesus. On the Mount of Transfiguration, God spoke from a cloud that surrounded those present and said, "This is my Son, whom I love. Listen to him!" (Mark 9:7).

The Lord God created us to have a personal relationship with Him and He wants us to spend time with Him. When we desire to know someone, there is no substitute for spending quality time together. The same is true of our relationship with God. In the Gospels, we learn that Jesus placed a priority on talking with His Father. Despite the demand on His time, Jesus often withdrew to places where He could be alone and pray.[11] What distractions prevent you from spending quality time alone with the Lord?

_____

_____

The more time we spend with God, the more He reveals Himself to us. But we need to communicate with Him—talking to Him through prayer, listening to Him through the Bible, and pondering His words through meditation. In your own words, rewrite Joshua 1:8 on the lines below.

_____

_____

_____

The Lord made it clear to Joshua that he was to read aloud God's Word, think about it, and obey it to be successful. Joshua was faithful to ask God's direction in the challenges he faced. They communicated with each other and had a personal relationship. Have you ever wondered how God spoke to Joshua? Did he have some of the same experiences that Moses had?

God speaks personally to us in different ways. He equips us with a spiritual ability to hear Him. Check the different ways the Lord has used to speak to you.

☐ sermons	☐ friends	☐ the Bible	☐ books
☐ teachers	☐ song lyrics	☐ movies	☐ strangers
☐ dreams	☐ in my mind	☐ radio	☐ Bible studies

How do you know when God is speaking to you? If you are listening to a sermon or lecture and the speaker addresses something that has been on your mind or says something that makes you sit up and take notice, the Spirit is speaking. When a verse seems to jump off a page as you read the Bible, He is getting your attention. Sometimes your heartbeat speeds up or seems to pound much harder, or your face and neck feel hot or flushed. If your senses are heightened and what is being said focuses on a concern you've had, God is talking to you. There are different physical symptoms that can occur, but if you sense that God is saying something to you personally, He probably is. If you question whether the words are really from God, make sure that what was said is consistent with the Bible and God's teaching. He never contradicts Himself. Prayerfully ask God to give you confirmation concerning that message.

It is remarkable the way God communicated with certain people in the Bible. Draw a line to match the people with the mode used by God to communicate.

Balaam	dream (Genesis 28)
Samuel	voice from burning bush (Exodus 3)
Jacob	donkey speaking words (Numbers 22)
Moses	voice at night (1 Samuel 3)
Shepherds	handwriting on the wall (Daniel 5)
Paul	voice from mountain top cloud (Mark 9)
King Belshazzar	angel of the Lord (Luke 2)
Peter, James & John	voice with heavenly light (Acts 9)

The Lord spoke with Moses face to face in the tent of meeting in the wilderness.[12] Moses requested that the Lord teach him His ways so he could know Him and find favor with Him (Exodus 33:13). Can you imagine having the Lord talk with you face to face? When Moses spent time with the Lord, his face became radiant (Exodus 34:34-35). Could it be that radiance was transferred from the physical presence of the divine? Moses took time, lots of time, to spend with God and consult with Him. How often do you talk with the Lord? Circle that which applies to you.

Only in emergencies	Once a week	Once a day
Never	When others pray	All the time

_____(other)

> "I am the good shepherd. I know my sheep and my sheep know me."
> John 10:14

God wants us to communicate with Him. We don't have to speak a formal prayer for God to listen; we can discuss our life with Him and talk with Him throughout the day. That is what many historical believers did – recorded in the Old and New Testament. God had many conversations with His people – from Adam and Eve to Noah, the patriarchs (Abraham, Isaac, and Jacob), Israel's leaders (Moses and Joshua), prophets like Samuel, and missionaries like the apostle Paul.

In 1Corinthians 8:3 we read, "But the man who loves God is known by God." These biblical people (mentioned above) loved God and communicated with Him. And God knew them.

Read John 10:14 in the inset. Judean shepherding was much different than it is today. Sheep would be with their shepherd for years and a deep relationship developed between them. Sheep recognize and listen only to their shepherd's voice. They will not respond to another person's voice. What did Jesus say in John 10:27? Fill in the blanks.

"My sheep _____ to my voice; I _____ them and

they _____ me."

David acknowledged the Lord as his shepherd in Psalm 23. We also need to be sheep who know our Shepherd's voice and listen to Him, and then follow Him. The longer we follow Jesus, the more readily we will recognize His voice. Sheep have a connection with their shepherd and they are valued by him. Jesus knows His sheep by name. Jesus knew His disciples' names before He even met them.

Read John 1:42, 47-48. Which two people did Jesus identify?_____

Jesus also called Zacchaeus by his name, and told him to come down out of the tree (Luke 19:1-6). Paul penned from his own experience, "...the Lord knows those who are his" (2 Timothy 2:19). Jesus had called him by name on his way to Damascus (Acts 9:3-6).

According to Revelation 3:5, Jesus declared, "I will never blot out his

_____ from the _____ _____ _____, but will

acknowledge his _____ before my Father and his angels."

Let's spend more time talking and listening to our Lord. Let's get to know Him better and develop that connection so we can trust Him more easily – like a sheep trusts its shepherd.

Prayer For Today:

Thank the Lord for loving you so much that He knows your name and wants a personal relationship with you.

Ask Him to help you recognize His voice so you can listen more attentively to Him.

_____

_____

_____

CHAPTER ONE DISCUSSION/REVIEW QUESTIONS

1. In what areas of your life do you have a hard time giving God complete control?

2. Why do you think we tend to do things our way and not trust God for the results of doing things His way?

3. What do you worry about?

4. According to Matthew 6:25-34 and Luke 12:22-31, what did Jesus say about worry? If you can, list other verses in the Bible that address worry.

5. What steps can we take to give our anxiousness to God and leave it with Him?

6. Try to remember and jot down a time when you felt God's love deep down inside. Can you describe that feeling?

7. How often do you read and study the Bible? (not enough, just enough, can't get enough) Why should it be a priority?

8. How many Bible verses do you think you have memorized? What caused you to memorize them? (school, Bible studies, just liked them…)

9. How does your life display the value of reading the Bible and obeying its principles?

10. What kinds of opposition seem to be most effective in your life to keep you from trusting God? Have you asked God for help?

11. Why don't we have to fear Satan?

12. What distractions keep you from spending quality time alone with the Lord?

13. What steps need to be taken for you to have a daily devotional time without interruption?

14. In what ways have you experienced God talking to you? How can you become a better listener?

Chapter Two: God's Power

Day One: Universe

Is God in control? Do you think there is anything that can occur in the entire universe that is outside of God's rule? If you think so, then you cannot completely trust Him for He does not have control and power over everything. But this is not the case because God created all and controls all. The Bible teaches that God created and governs the universe – all things (visible and invisible), creatures, and men. Read John 1:3 and fill in the blanks below.

"Through _____ _____ things were made; without him _____ was made that has been made."

What does Hebrews 11:3 reveal about the universe?

_____

_____

What did Paul proclaim in Colossians 1:16-17?

_____

_____

God is not only the Creator, He is also the Sustainer of the world—in Him all things hold together. In Hebrews 1:3 we read, "The Son...sustaining all things by his powerful word." God holds and maintains the world He created - day by day and year by year. He keeps all the systems working. He causes the earth to continue rotating on its axis once every 23 hours and 56 minutes, tilted at 23.5° to cause our seasons, and revolving around the sun that is 93 million miles away. The sun is 99% of the mass of our solar system that is located inside the Milky Way Galaxy, which is only a tiny part of the universe. Are you getting an idea of how big our God is? The moon stays an average 238,881.81 miles away from the earth and its rotation is once every 27.3 days, the exact time it takes to revolve around the earth (so you never see the back side of the moon from the earth). The moon is responsible for the tides of our oceans. Do the details of how our universe operates astound you?

Think about the evolutionists' theory of how the world evolved out of nothing. This theory cannot be possible because the first Law of Thermodynamics states that energy can be changed from one form to another, but it cannot be created or destroyed. The total amount of energy and matter in the universe remains constant, merely changing from one form to another.

The 2nd Law of Thermodynamics reveals that whenever energy is exchanged, if no energy enters or leaves the system, the potential energy of the state will always be less than that of the initial state. When things are left alone, they weaken or deteriorate. They do not gain strength and come together.

These laws (statements of scientific fact that are invariable) give scientific proof that the Big Bang theory is false. There is also an issue of entropy, which is a measure of disorder or the degree of randomness. Therefore, the world didn't gradually happen on its own; it took a miracle. God created it and He sustains it.

As we become more educated, new scientific facts concur with the Bible. Scientists are realizing that the complexity of the human cell has no other origin than intelligent design. And the Bible footnotes give much interesting insight. From Colossians 1:16-17:

> …all the rulers, powers, thrones, and authorities of both the spiritual and physical worlds were created by and are under the authority of Christ himself. This includes…the spiritual world…Christ has no equal and no rival. He is the Lord of all. God is not only the Creator of the world, but he is also its Sustainer. In him, everything is held together, protected, and prevented from disintegrating into chaos. Because Christ is the Sustainer of all life, none of us is independent from him. We…must daily trust him for protecting us, caring for us, and sustaining us.[13]

God not only sustains the earth and heavenly bodies, He sustains His people. "For in him we live and move and have our being" (Acts 17:28). Since creation, how has God shown His active control over what He created in space? Write the answers on the lines provided after the reference.

Genesis 7:11-12 _____

Genesis 19:24 _____

Exodus 10:21-23 _____

Joshua 10:13-14 _____

James 5:17-18 _____

From the springs of the great deep to the clouds, sun, moon, stars, and atmosphere around the earth - everything obeys the Creator's desires.

These passages teach us that God intentionally intervenes and does supernatural things that no one else can control. From the springs of the great deep to the clouds, sun, moon, stars, and atmosphere around the earth – everything obeys the Creator's desires. The author of Psalm 148:1-6 wrote about creation praising the Lord. Draw a line to match the verses with the created entities that praise God.

Verse 1	sun, moon, shining stars
Verse 2	highest heavens, waters above the skies
Verse 3	heavens, heights above
Verse 4	angels, heavenly hosts

> "Praise the Lord, you his angels, you mighty ones who do his bidding, who obey his word. Praise the Lord, all his heavenly hosts, you his servants who do his will."
> Psalm 103:20-21

In Psalm 148:5-6 we read, "…for he commanded and they were created. He set them in place for ever and ever." Again we see God's incredible power with just His words. God's words set the world in place. Did you notice that in Genesis 1, it is recorded that "God said" and it was so?

God challenged Job with questions about the beginning of the world. Take time to read Job 38 for we cannot comprehend everything that God did as He created the world. It surely puts us in our place to be reminded that God is sovereign over all He made – the entire universe. He knows everything that occurs in the skies above and on the earth below. He is still in control; God's power is ruling in areas we can't even see. We don't often think about the spiritual world or the invisible world (out of sight = out of mind?), but God is sovereign over that, too. Read Psalm 103:20-21 in the inset. What do the Lord's angels and all His heavenly hosts do?

_____

_____

God creates, rules, and sustains; yet, He has given man dominion over the earth. How are you taking care of the earth God gave you? Do you litter? Recycle? Do you ever look up into the sky at night and gaze at the moon and stars? Have you seen meteor showers? Have you witnessed solar or lunar eclipses? When have you been awed by observing God's creation in the skies? "The heavens declare the glory of God; the skies proclaim the work of his hands" (Psalm 19:1). The Creator made and governs the physical and spiritual worlds.

Prayer For Today:

Thank God for His magnificent creation and that He still sustains it.

Ask God to overwhelm you as you look up in the sky at night and think about how detailed and vast His world is.

_____

_____

_____

One month after simultaneously enrolling my son into a Christian pre-school and a special education school, our family went camping and was sitting around the campfire at night. My son stared at the sky for a long while and then recited as he continued gazing, "In the beginning, God created the heavens and the earth. God saw 'aaall' that He had made and it was very good." Even a handicapped five-year-old can sincerely praise the Lord for His creation. How great is our God!

Day Two: Nature

Yesterday we were reminded of how powerful our God is, how vast and immeasurable creation is, and that God is still involved in what He made, particularly in the sky. Today, let's look at God's sovereignty over nature. There is a lot of biblical evidence that God intervened with the earth's elements. Below are different elements of nature used in miracles by Him. The recorded events are exciting and worth the effort of looking up the references. Briefly summarize the miracle on the line provided.

fire _____ (Daniel 3:25-27)

_____ (1 Kings 18:38)

rivers _____ (2 Kings 2:8,14)

_____ (Exodus 7:17)

cloud _____ (Exodus 13:21-22)

seas _____ (Exodus 14:21-22)

rocks _____ (Exodus 17:6)

earthquakes _____ (Numbers 16:30-33)

dew _____ (Judges 6:37-40)

trees _____ (Matthew 21:19)

wind _____ (Mark 4:37-39)

There are many more examples of God using the earth's elements to create supernatural events. His purposeful miracles were attention-getters, and used for teaching, judgment, guidance, and provision. Additional references of God's active power are: Exodus 3:2, Exodus 40:34-38, Numbers 16:35, and Joshua 3:15-17.

Which of the above miracles do you wish to have seen?_____

All of these biblical evidences of God's power and activity in the world support His total sovereignty. He is able to do anything – supernatural to us – and that is what makes Him God. He is not frivolous with His interventions but used all these elements for specific reasons which aided His purpose. A miracle is a divine act unexplainable by the laws of nature. Miracles defy scientific explanation. Why did God perform so many miracles in the Old Testament? Let's look at Psalm 78:4, 7:

> …We will tell the next generation the praiseworthy deeds of the Lord, his power, and the wonders he has done. Then they would put their trust in God and would not forget his deeds but would keep his commands.

God produced miraculous events to teach His children that He alone is God; He is able to do anything and rules over everything.

We are encouraged and comforted through our difficult times by remembering God's help through His miracles in the past. When God displayed His power to the Egyptians and Israelites through the ten plagues, He was showing them that He is the only true God. (The Egyptians worshipped many false gods.) The Lord God Almighty caused miraculous events to educate His people about His power so they would worship, fear, and trust Him alone. Much later, memories of those miracles helped some Israelites when they started to doubt.

While God performed incredible deeds to teach His children necessary lessons about His character, He also took supernatural measures to provide for their needs and to discipline them. Israel was becoming a nation and was still learning about their God - their holy and just God who loved His people, who provided for and protected His children. He wanted to be their only God and for Israel to be His people.

Miraculous events did not stop after the Old Testament era, (BC). In the New Testament times, Jesus was conceived by the Holy Spirit. When He started His earthly ministry, Jesus performed miracles to accompany His words. He was teaching new concepts, and God gave Him authority to prove His words were true and to support His claims.

Read John 14:11 in the inset. What does Jesus want us to believe?

_____

_____

_____

"Believe me when I say that I am in the Father and the Father is in me; or at least believe on the evidence of the miracles themselves."
John 14:11

People took notice. Jesus used His power to heal, provide, forgive, convince, and educate people. He got everyone's attention; He also wanted their hearts.

And now we have the Bible that recorded all of these historical, supernatural events to teach us about the Lord. Read John 20:30-31 below:

> Jesus did many other miraculous signs in the presence of his disciples,
> which are not recorded in this book. But these are written that you may
> believe that Jesus is the Christ, the Son of God, and that by believing you
> may have life in his name.

The miracles were not ends in themselves. They always had a purpose. Does God still perform miracles? Yes, He does. Miracles like separating the Red Sea so a whole nation can walk through? Not lately - modern transportation has eliminated that situational need. But God continues to work in many miraculous ways and has a plan that He is still executing.

Have you ever asked God for a miracle? _____ Have you experienced a miracle in your life or witnessed one in another person's life? _____ Why do you think God performed the miracle? What did you learn from it?

_____

_____

_____

Every supernatural event displays God's power and supreme control – His sovereignty – over nature. "I will remember the deeds of the Lord; yes, I will remember your miracles of long ago. I will meditate on all your works and consider all your mighty deeds. Your ways, O God, are holy. What god is so great as our God? You are the God who performs miracles; you display your power among the peoples" (Psalm 77:11-14).

Prayer For Today:

Thank God that He has revealed to us His power and control over nature in both the Old and New Testament. Thank Him that He still is active in our world today.

Ask the Lord to help you remember His miracles when you need encouragement or courage.

_____

_____

_____

Day Three: Creatures

Many years ago, I put my first lovable pet – a sheltie dog – to sleep forever. He had kidney disease and two pinched nerves, and became sick. After sharing eleven years of my life with "Rocky," I couldn't bear the thought of him suffering, and had him euthanized. I never thought I would be the type of person to get attached to a dog, but I did. I also took him for granted and ended up missing him for many years.

As I reflect upon my dog, I remember first and foremost how happy he was to see me and receive personal attention from me. I'd just call his name once and he'd be right there, watching me and listening. He loved me unconditionally, was faithful, easily forgave me, and was always waiting for me when I returned home. Isn't that similar to what God does? He loves to hear from us, wants us to talk to Him and have undivided, quality time with Him. He loves us unconditionally, is always faithful, and forgives us repeatedly. God listens to us whenever we call out to Him, and He'll be waiting for us when we go to our heavenly home.

Animals can direct or point us to God. The uniqueness and diversity of species, breeds, and personalities are no accident. They reveal God's creativity and glory. God made living creatures on the fifth day of creation. In Genesis 1:21, 25 we read:

> So God created the great creatures of the sea and every living and moving thing with which the water teems, according to their kinds, and every winged bird according to its kind. And God saw that it was good. God made the wild animals according to their kinds, the livestock according to their kinds, and all the creatures that move along the ground according to their kinds. And God saw that it was good.

It is interesting that one can read a familiar passage in the Bible and see something new or different every time. For instance, did you ever notice that a serpent "spoke" to Eve (Genesis 3:11)? Did some of the creatures have the ability to talk like humans? Did a serpent originally have legs and feet? His curse was that he'd have to crawl on his belly and eat dust.[14]

Animals have useful purposes. Historically, horses, donkeys, and camels provided transportation, and oxen were used for labor. Sheep, goats, and cattle were livestock to be eaten. After the flood, God gave man every creature, bird, and fish to be eaten. Read Genesis 1:29-30 and Genesis 9:2-3. Notice that everything created was good. Animals were not created to eat each other; they were given "every green plant for food." They became enemies after the fall of man, when sin affected all of creation. (I became enemies with mosquitoes at a very young age!) God's perfect design in creating all the fish, birds, and creatures is revealed in the Bible, and His power and sovereignty over them are easily seen. Write the supernatural event involving these creatures on the lines provided for each of the references given.

livestock - Exodus 9:3-6 _____

birds - Exodus 16:13 _____

birds - 1 Kings 17:6 _____

bears - 2 Kings 2:24 _____

snakes - Numbers 21:6 _____

donkey - Numbers 22:28-30 _____

lions - Daniel 6:21-24 _____

fish - Matthew 17:27 _____

   - Mark 6:41-44 _____

Additionally, God caused a great fish to swallow the prophet Jonah and later vomit him back onto dry land (Jonah 1 & 2). Jesus provided the disciples with a miraculous catch of fish on two separate occasions (Luke 5:6; John 21:11). And God plagued the Egyptians with frogs, gnats, flies, and locusts (Exodus 8 & 10). I am fascinated how God uses all of His creation, even insects, to accomplish His purposes.

If God can speak through a donkey, do you think He could speak through you too? Do you trust Him enough to give you the words to say? _____ How many opportunities to give the gospel or share your faith have you let pass by? _____ Have you ever defended another Christian who was being mocked or criticized for his faith? What excuses have you used to justify not saying anything? Check all that apply.

☐ Not my business

☐ Don't know what to say

☐ Don't want to be ridiculed

☐ I might cause a strain in a friendship

☐ I might lose an opportunity for a promotion or even my job

☐ I stutter and stumble over my words when I'm nervous

☐ I have bad breath and don't want to open my mouth

☐ _____ (another reason)

Do our coworkers and neighbors know that we love the Lord by the things we say and do? Most of us have failed God in this way. Nevertheless, we must not be fearful to express, explain, or defend our faith. "Do not worry about what to say or how to say it. At that time you will be given what to say, for it will not be you speaking, but the Spirit of your Father speaking through you" (Matthew 10:19-20).

God equips us to do His work; He doesn't necessarily call those who are already equipped. The only ability God is looking for in us is our availability. He works in inexperienced people so He can be glorified. The Lord doesn't want us to take the credit but to depend on Him for what we need, (including the right words to say). Then we can give Him all the glory. The Lord counseled, "I am with you; that is all you need. My power shows up best in weak people."[15] Paul proclaimed in Philippians 4:13, "I can do all things through Christ who strengthens me." Peter and John were defending themselves in front of the rulers, elders, and teachers of the law who "when they saw the courage of Peter and John and realized that they were unschooled, ordinary men, they were astonished and they took note that these men had been with Jesus" (Acts 4:13). Trust the Holy Spirit to speak through you so you may be a blessing to others and glorify God.

God uses animals and people in ways that glorify Him.

While the Lord God has given us dominion over the creatures, He has done miraculous things with varieties of them, and all are subject to His wishes and plans. These miracles give evidence of God's power, authority, and sovereignty over His creation. He is the same God then as He is now[16] and He is still ruling over the heavens, earth, and His creatures.

Prayer For Today:

Thank God that His creation has given you pleasure (especially if you have a pet or enjoy zoos).

Ask the Holy Spirit to give you the right words to say and guidance when to speak or keep quiet.

_____

_____

_____

Day Four: People

Does God truly control the circumstances of our lives or do "bad" things randomly happen to us because we live in a sinful world? Both statements are true. According to the Bible, God is sovereign over people. He allows individuals to make choices and gives them free will; however, He can and will intervene in their lives to accomplish a specific purpose. God created man, so it isn't difficult to believe that He can do anything else to him. God healed many diseases and disabilities, caused the deaths of certain people, and even raised people from the dead. Furthermore, God has intervened in men's actions, and in less visible ways, in their minds. In Proverbs 19:21 we read, "Many are the plans in a man's heart, but it is the Lord's purpose that prevails." Look up these next two verses and fill in the blanks.

Proverbs 16:9   "In his _____ a _____ _____ his

course, but the _____ _____ his steps."

Lamentations 3:37 "Who can _____ and have it _____ if the Lord has not _____ it?"

Many other Bible passages support this concept of control, and an incident recorded in the Bible validates these verses. King Balak hired a popular pagan diviner, named Balaam, to curse Israel. As stated in Numbers 23:5, "The Lord put a message in Balaam's mouth." Thus, Balaam could only speak blessings instead of curses, which infuriated King Balak (recorded in Numbers 24). God has the power to control the words coming out of our mouths!

If God has control over people, how are we to act when our immediate future can be decided by someone else? Do we believe that God has power over the heart and mind of that person? What if someone is out to ruin our reputation or make us the target of their hate? Can we ask God to change the minds of those individuals so they don't pursue their harmful intent?

The Bible's answer is yes. What if someone succeeds in their evil plans, even after our prayer that God will intervene to keep it from happening? We must still trust God because He has allowed it for a reason. "The king's heart is in the hand of the Lord; he directs it like a water-course wherever he pleases" (Proverbs 21:1). It is as easy as moving the pipes of an irrigation system to direct the flow of water. God rules over every person, believer, and unbeliever, and that includes those who have authority over us.

> "And we know that in all things God works for the good of those who love Him, who have been called according to His purpose." Romans 8:28

This concept is difficult to accept when one has been treated unfairly. Our family could see events unfold that were manipulated and dishonest, and we did our best to trust God amid our disappointment. Why does God allow the deceitful guy to become prosperous and the good guy to lose his job? We may never know.

When a family's wage earner is unemployed with no immediate prospect for a job, his faith is tested as he pays the bills and seeks work. Yet, in our family's history, we've experienced a faithful God who has given better jobs to replace the ones taken away. We do not know why God restrains some enemies but allows others to carry out their evil plans. But we do know that He is in control and is working behind the scenes where we can't see Him. We also know that God works for our good when we love and serve Him. Read Romans 8:28 in the inset.

When have you seen God take a bad situation and turn it into something good?

_____

When my daughter received a rejection letter to her application into a physical therapy program, we were surprised and distressed. She had no plan B. After praying Romans 8:28, incredible timing of situations occurred which resulted in her acceptance into a master's program at the university of her choice with a graduate assistantship. Unforeseen benefits surfaced; our daughter received a master's degree without any additional debt and the additional education helped her in several ways when she was in the PT program later.

There are biblical evidences of God's intervening work in the hearts and minds of believers and unbelievers. What did God do in these passages?

Exodus 4:21; 9:12   _____

Deuteronomy 2:30   _____

Ezra 1:1,5   _____

Ezra 6:22   _____

Daniel 1:9   _____

Look at the verbs in these verses. God *empowered* Moses and *hardened* Pharaoh's heart; God *made* King Sidon's spirit stubborn and heart obstinate; God *filled* the Israelites with joy by *changing* the king's attitude; the Lord *moved* the king's heart and also *moved* the hearts of family heads and priests; and God *caused* the official to show favor and sympathy. God is active in people's lives; He generates outcomes that accomplish His plans and answers prayers. Notice that God had a reason for making King Sidon's spirit stubborn – to give his nation into the Israelites' hands. God hardened Pharaoh's evil heart, preventing the Israelites from leaving, so that He could demonstrate His power to the Israelites through the plagues. God always has a purpose for His interventions.

We may not understand why negative incidents happen, but we need to trust that God loves us and is in control, carrying out His plans. No one can do anything nor can any event take place outside the boundary of God's rule. And there is no plan of God that can be messed up. Job confessed, "I know that you can do all things; no plan of yours can be thwarted" (Job 42:2).

Do the sinful actions of man affect God's plans? Let's look at Genesis 50:20.

> *Even though God allows sinful actions to occur, He uses them to accomplish His will.*

Joseph said to his brothers, "You intended to harm me but God intended it for good to accomplish what is now being done, the saving of many lives." Man's sin will not alter God's plans. Even though God allows sinful actions to occur, He uses them to accomplish His will. Remember that no one can thwart God's plans.

Therefore, as we experience rough times, be mindful that life's uncertainties are like weaving a tapestry where underneath it looks a mess, but when it is finished and turned over, we see a beautiful picture. As we trust God, life may seem confusing now, but we will see the wonderful outcome later.

What evidence do you see – past or present – of God's involvement in your life? Make a list of the times God's power was noticeable to you. I suggest starting this list on the last "Personal Notes" page located in the back of this workbook. As you take the time to think about your life (ask God to bring those times to your mind), write down every experience you can remember and keep a running list. During the course of this study, perhaps more events will come to your mind and you can continue to record them. After the study is completed, tear that page out and keep it in your Bible as a reminder of God's great love for you.

If you have a personal relationship with the Lord, there will be signs of God working in your life. Keep that list available to look at when you need encouragement. It helps every time, for God will remind you that He is active, in control, and answers prayers.

Prayer For Today:

Thank God that He is sovereign and very aware of your circumstances and able to work things out for your good.

Ask God to cause you to remember how He has helped you in the past so you can be encouraged in your present.

_____

_____

_____

Day Five: Nations/Government Leaders

> "…O Lord God of our fathers, are you not the God who is in heaven? You rule over all the kingdoms of the nations. Power and might are in your hand and no one can withstand you."
> 2 Chronicles 20:6

How much involvement does God have over nations and their government? Terrorist attacks, wars, hatred, and nuclear threats exist between nations. Is God watching all of this from heaven and sighing with disgust? Is He involved at all? Read 2 Chronicles 20:6 in the inset. God is sovereign over every single nation, ruling over all of them, and directing events and decisions to fulfill His purpose. He allows (without liking) many of man's decisions to proceed, along with their consequences. He has a permissive will besides a perfect will. When Israel wanted their first earthly king, God permitted it after they ignored His warning.[17]

Let's look at these next passages and read what the Bible reveals concerning God's involvement over governments and their leaders. What does God do?

Daniel 4:17b   _____

Daniel 4:31-33 _____

Proverbs 16:33 _____

Proverbs 21:31 _____

We read that God decides who rules in some nations' governments. He sets the length of the leader's reign, and selectively controls decisions that the rulers make. And God may determine the victories and defeats between nations.

Some of Israel's historical battles consisted of God defeating their enemies for them. One time, Jehoshaphat was told that the battle he was facing wasn't his but God's.[18] Israel wouldn't even have to fight - only witness the deliverance the Lord would give them. God orchestrated the opposing armies' deaths, and when Jehoshaphat and his army arrived at the place where God told them to go, they found dead bodies lying on the ground. Instead of fighting, they spent three days collecting all the plunder. Wouldn't you like God to fight your battles like that?

Understanding God's reign and power over past nations and leaders gives us assurance that He's also ruling over our present ones.

Gideon, along with 300 men, blew trumpets around the Midianite camp. God guided the Midianites to turn on each other with their swords, and whoever was left, fled.[19]

It's amusing that God caused the Egyptians to give the Israelites their gold, jewelry, and other valuables when they left Egypt. "The Lord made the Egyptians favorably disposed toward the people and they gave them what they asked for, so they plundered the Egyptians" (Exodus 12:36). The Egyptians hated the Israelites and treated them unjustly, yet God made that nation of people have the disposition to give their enemy their riches.

Later in history when Israel was unfaithful, God allowed Israel's opponents victory in war, bringing about Israel's deportation and captivity as punishment. God has intervened in various nations' victories and defeats, bringing blessings or enslavement to serve His purpose.

God planned for all of these specific events to be recorded in the Bible for our benefit - to teach us to trust and obey Him. Understanding God's reign and power over past nations and leaders gives us assurance that He's also ruling over our present ones.

We have seen governments working without any fear of God or without any thought of accountability to Him, and other nations destroyed because of their immorality. Yet, behind the scenes, God has been watching and ruling to carry out His plans. The unjust events that led to the crucifixion of Jesus Christ demonstrate this. The Jewish leaders produced false witnesses and called for Jesus' death even though He did no wrong. The government held unlawful court sessions to convict Jesus. But Jesus knew God's plan and together they allowed it all to happen, even though it didn't appear that way. Read what Jesus said as recorded in Matthew 26:53-54.

Do you think I cannot call on my Father, and he will at once put at my disposal more than twelve legions of angels? But how then would the Scriptures be fulfilled that say it must happen in this way?

Peter had cut off the high priest's servant's ear after Jesus was arrested. He didn't understand what had to happen. But after Jesus' death and resurrection, it made sense. In fact, Peter's prayer recognized God's foreknowledge, plans, and power:

Indeed Herod and Pontius Pilate met together with the Gentiles and the people of Israel in this city to conspire against your holy servant Jesus, whom you anointed. They did what your power and will had decided beforehand should happen. (Acts 4:27-28)

Similarly, the events today may appear that God is not in control, but He is. Our nation is under God because He is sovereign; He rules over the country whether we acknowledge and obey Him or not. Even if we can't perceive God's interventions in the nations at this present time, He is no less active today than He was in the Old or New Testament days. "The Lord foils the plans of the nations; he thwarts the purposes of the peoples" (Psalm 33:10). God is still involved in governments – the time or length of a leader's rule, the decision making (wise and foolish), granting victories and defeats in war, and using ungodly nations to carry out His will.

Why do you think God allows opposition to Christianity and the persecution of its followers in so many nations? Attending a church, reading the Bible, and speaking about Jesus is breaking a law and worthy of prison or death in certain countries. Many people risk their lives for their faith.

How many governments in our world actually fear the Lord? In America, the basis of morality (the Bible) has been diluted, undermined, and ignored. Christians are viewed as intolerant to the nation's sins and are increasingly disrespected and persecuted. In Psalm 33:12 we read, "Blessed is the nation whose God is the Lord." Historically, God blessed the nation whose leader feared the Lord and led the people in doing what was good and right in God's eyes. And He still will. What fears do you have about your nation's future? _____

There are many problems concerning the governments on this earth, but none outside of God's knowledge or control. Are you doing anything about your fears? King David professed, "In God I trust; I will not be afraid. What can man do to me?" (Psalm 56:11). We need to trust God when foolish and ungodly decisions are made. Christians have a responsibility to pray for the leaders and lawmakers of their government. Pray for those people to fear God, seek His help and direction, and make wise decisions. God advises us to pray for our leaders, so our prayers must make a difference. Moses' prayer saved Israel from disaster[20] and the Ninevites were spared from destruction after they repented.[21]

The apostle Paul wrote, "I urge…that requests, prayers, intercession and thanksgiving be made for everyone – for kings and all those in authority…" (1 Timothy 2:1-2). So who has authority over you? Parents? Teachers? Bosses? Government leaders? Write down your government leaders' names (find out if you don't know them).

Town/city/county _____

State senators _____

State representatives _____

State Governor _____

President and Vice-President _____

Supreme Court judges _____

Will you pray for your leaders? I've found myself praying Psalm 109:8 for some!

Prayer For Today:

Thank God that He is still involved in the nations today and that nothing happens outside of His control.

Ask God to give wisdom to our nation's leaders and cause them to make godly decisions.

_____

_____

_____

CHAPTER TWO DISCUSSION/REVIEW QUESTIONS

1. When have you been awed by God's creation?

2. Have you ever experienced a miracle in your life or in someone close to you? If so, what did you learn from it?

3. How open are you to sharing your faith with others? Do you trust God enough to give you the words to say?

4. Are you prepared to give a defense or reason for the faith you have? Read 1Peter 3:15. If not, what steps are needed to get prepared? If yes, how did you prepare?

5. Do you think the people you work with or your neighbors know you are a Christian? Share your reasons for your answer.

6. When has God turned a bad experience or event of yours into something good?

7. When you are going through a difficult time, what helps you keep your faith and not despair?

8. How do the sinful actions of man affect God's plans?

9. Why do you think God allows so many nations to be hostile to the gospel of Jesus Christ?

10. What is your favorite event in the Bible that displays God's power?

11. How often do you pray for your leaders? Mention your local and state leaders' names and pray for them at the close of your session.

12. Share a time when God has intervened and helped you. Continue making your list of God's active participation in your life. Maybe someone else's experience may trigger a memory of an event of your own.

I encourage you to make a list of times that God has intervened in your life. What events in your life were more than coincidences? What accidents did you narrowly escape? When did God answer your prayer? How did He turn that bad event into something good?

Your recorded entries will create an awareness of God's activity throughout your life. If your memory fails you, ask God for help in recalling His interventions. Then keep the list handy so events can be added when they are remembered and as they occur.

Furthermore, God wants us to do more than remember. He wants us to share our stories. "Declare His glory among the nations, his marvelous deeds among all peoples" (Psalm 96:3). "Give thanks to the Lord, call on his name; make known among the nations what he has done. Sing to him, sing praise to him; tell of all his wonderful acts" (1 Chronicles 16:8-9).

When we are alert for occasions to tell others about God, it is amazing how often the opportunity presents itself. Discussing how the Lord rescues, heals, protects, and provides reminds us of how loving and powerful He is. It encourages others and glorifies God when we make known what He has done for us. Remembering His active presence in our lives makes us more mindful of and thankful for our blessings. As the song lyrics suggest, "Count your many blessings, name them one by one, count your many blessings, see what God has done."

So what has God done for you lately?

Chapter Three: God's Knowledge

Have you ever felt all alone or lonely, even in a crowd? Do you feel misunderstood or think that no one knows the real you? Fill in the blanks of Psalm 147:5.

"Great is our Lord and mighty in _____; his

_____ has _____ _____."

> "Before I formed you in the womb I knew you, before you were born, I set you apart..."
> Jeremiah 1:5

How is it possible that the Lord understands us? If He hasn't experienced what we have, can He really know how we feel? The answer is yes because God created us. He is the master designer of our bodies and knows how everything works – even our minds. I can't figure out why I do the things I do or even why I feel a certain way at times, yet God knows me better than I know myself. His understanding has no limit.

Read Jeremiah 1:5 in the inset. When did the Lord first know us?

_____

_____

God told Jeremiah that He knew him even before He formed him in his mother's womb. David attributed his existence to God in Psalm 139:13, "For you created my inmost being; you knit me together in my mother's womb." In the Hebrew language, "inmost being" refers to the innermost center of emotions and moral sensitivity, which God tests and examines when He searches a person's mind and heart.[22] Jeremiah was told that before he left the womb, God had a plan for his life. Our Maker not only designs our beings, but also sets us apart to serve Him. "'For I know the plans I have for you,' declares the Lord..." (Jeremiah 29:11). David proclaimed, "Your eyes saw my unformed body. All the days ordained for me were written in your book before one of them came to be."[23]

Since God created us, He knows every part of our bodies and He understands our personalities. Whenever we are in pain or are ill, God knows exactly what is causing the problem. After all these years, scientists and doctors still don't have all the answers to how the human body works. But the Lord does; moreover, He's the Great Physician who is able to heal us. Draw a line to match these verses with God's knowledge about us:

Our weaknesses	Psalm 44:21
Our future	Psalm 94:11
Our hearts	Jeremiah 29:11
Our secrets	Matthew 6:31-32
Our thoughts	Luke 12:7
Our lies	Luke 16:15
Our needs	Romans 8:26
The number of hairs on our head	2 Corinthians 11:31

Let's face it. If God knows our heart,[24] the number of hairs on our heads, and our future, He knows more about us than we know of ourselves. So that is why we should trust Him. He is infinite in wisdom and does not make any mistakes. Look up these verses about God's wisdom and knowledge, and fill in the blanks.

Isaiah 55:9 "As the _____ are _____ than the _____, so are _____ _____ _____ than _____ _____ and my _____ than your _____."

1 Corinthians 1:25 "For the _____ of _____ is _____ than _____ _____, and the _____ of God is _____ than man's _____."

Colossians 2:3 "Christ, in whom are hidden all the _____ of _____ and _____."

We read in these verses that God's wisdom and knowledge are valued, even considered treasures. When we value and trust God's wisdom, submit to His way over our ways, He rewards us both in the present and in the future.

God blessed me when He provided a job for me. He looked out for my health, something I didn't really think about. I wanted to work in the medical field, but I didn't have enough strength to lift patients without hurting myself. I was focused on working in hospitals or nursing homes, yet questioned my ability. Since God knows me better than I know myself, He coordinated events that led to an offer from a dentist office. He made sure I had patients that were mostly healthy, not sick, thus protecting my weakened immune system that I forgot about. God gave me what I desired—a part-time medical job—and because of His wisdom and my lack of it, He also protected my health and strength. Yeah, God is good.

In what ways has our all-knowing God protected you or kept you safe? (Any near-accidents, life-threatening situations, weather-related close calls or dangerous encounters? Or maybe not so extreme, but just constant protection against illnesses or injuries?)

_____

_____

_____

> *God has infinite knowledge, but we have finite minds that simply cannot comprehend any more than what God reveals to us.*

God's wisdom is more than just knowledge and understanding of humans. He is Creator and Sustainer of the world, Provider, Healer, Savior, the Trinity, and the list goes on. There are aspects of God (and life in general) that we will never comprehend. My mind has a difficult time with the idea of eternity, that there is no end. As much as my intellect can grasp, I believe and accept the concept of the Trinity - God is the Father, Son, and Holy Spirit - but cannot fully understand the 3-in-1 design. God has infinite knowledge but we have finite (limited) minds that simply cannot comprehend any more than what God reveals to us. If we knew and understood everything, there would be no need for faith or trust. That is why Jesus tells us to come to Him as little children who are humble and very trusting of their parents, and to trust Him without reservation. Read Matthew 18:3 in the inset. According to Jesus, what will we miss if we don't change and become like little children and trust God?

_____

Young children believe without understanding; likewise, we must believe, trust, and have faith in Jesus, even though we cannot comprehend everything. Faith is driving on an old, long and narrow bridge when you cannot see its end. God wants unconditional trust without our knowing what lies ahead or all the answers. Although we cannot understand our Maker, we can take comfort that because He formed and made us, He knows every part of our being. We can rejoice that God's knowledge is complete – that He designed us, knows us intimately, and understands us. God knows what is best for each one of us and that is why we can trust Him with our lives.

> "And he said; I tell you the truth, unless you change and become like little children, you will never enter the kingdom of heaven."
> Matthew 18:3

Prayer For Today:

Thank God for His immeasurable wisdom and that He knows you better than you know yourself.

Ask God to help you humble yourself to trust Him without hesitation, as a little child trusts without knowing or understanding everything.

_____

_____

_____

Day Two: Knowledge and Understanding

Have you ever experienced a mental blank - when you can't remember a person's name as you're introducing them (and you know them well)? Have you lost your train of thought midway through speaking a sentence? Or perhaps you have struggled to think of the right word to use when expressing an opinion.

Besides being in these humbling situations, I admit that my vocabulary knowledge is limited and that I've forgotten almost everything I learned in college. I'm becoming absent-minded because sometimes I walk into a room and can't remember the reason for going there. My mind is like lightning – one brilliant flash and then it's gone!

In the previous lesson, we were reminded of God's unlimited knowledge and wisdom. Today, we will address man's knowledge and wisdom. First, let's look at the difference between the words "knowledge" and "wisdom." Knowledge is: the state or fact of knowing (to recognize, acknowledge, be familiar with), awareness, the sum of what has been learned or discovered. Wisdom is: the ability to make good use of knowledge, the ability to recognize right from wrong (discernment), good judgment, being shrewd.[25] Man can have intellect or knowledge, and have earned several advanced degrees, but still not possess wisdom. Age does not guarantee wisdom either. Wisdom is more than knowledge. So how do we become wise? Job penned:

> I thought, 'Age should speak; advanced years should teach wisdom.'
> But it is the spirit in a man, the breath of the Almighty, that gives him understanding. (Job 32:7-8)

The words "spirit" and "breath" refer to the Spirit of God. In other words, it is the Holy Spirit that gives man understanding. This word "understanding" is taken from the Hebrew word "biyn" which is defined as "insight, closely related to wisdom." The word does not refer to the mere accumulation of data, but superior knowledge. One must know how to use information wisely.[26] Knowledge, understanding, and discernment are different components of wisdom. What does the Bible say about desiring wisdom?

Proverbs 4:7 "Wisdom is supreme; therefore _____

_____. Though it cost all you have, _____

_____."

Proverbs 8:11 "For _____ is more _____ than

rubies, and _____ you desire can compare with her."

We learn that wisdom has worth and is valuable to have. Whom do you consider to be wise?

_____

Why do you think they are wise? _____

_____

"If any of you lacks wisdom, he should ask God, who gives generously to all without finding fault, and it will be given to him." James 1:5

If wisdom is desirable, and it is given by God, how does one attain it from Him? Read James 1:5 in the inset. Is it really that easy? Just ask God for wisdom, seek it, and He will give it to us? Fill in the blank to complete Proverbs 2:6.

"For the _____ _____

_____, and from his

mouth come _____ and

_____."

An NIV footnote for this verse explains this further:

Wisdom comes in two ways: it is a God-given gift and also the result of an energetic search. Wisdom's starting point is God and his revealed Word, the source of 'knowledge and understanding.' In that sense, wisdom is his gift to us. But he gives it only to those who earnestly seek it. But because God's wisdom is hidden from the rebellious and foolish, it takes effort to find it and use it. The pathway to wisdom is strenuous. When we are on the path, we discover that true wisdom is God's and that he will guide us and reward our sincere and persistent search.[27]

When we obey God's guidelines for living (that are recorded in the Bible), we learn why He gives them and appreciate the gained insight. If we earnestly seek wisdom and ask God for it, He will give it to us, even generously. As easy as that sounds, the Lord—who searches our minds and hearts—looks at our motives for wanting wisdom. If we possess the right motives, He will answer our requests. God generously rewarded Solomon who asked for wisdom and knowledge. His story is recorded in 1Kings 3:3-13, 4:29-34, and in 2Chronicles 1:6-13. Read these passages in your Bible. What exactly did Solomon request and for what purpose? (1 Kings 3:9)

_____

_____

The 2nd Chronicles passage reveals that Solomon asked God for wisdom and knowledge to help him lead God's people. Solomon had the right motive. And God's response was not only to give Solomon a wise and discerning heart, but to make him the wisest man who ever lived on earth. Furthermore, God gave him wealth, riches, and honor above all other kings in his lifetime.[28] Men of all nations came to listen to Solomon's wisdom. Now that's an answer to an honorable request! Have you ever asked God for wisdom or for understanding and insight? _____ If so, did you receive it?

Paul confirmed God's goodness in answering prayers; he wrote that God is able to do immeasurably more than all we ask or imagine (Ephesians 3:20). Do we set our expectations too low?

My husband took a temporary job that required him to work out of state during the week and to fly home on weekends. We had three school-aged children who were actively involved in sports and school activities, and I selfishly wanted my husband home to help me with the kids. I should have been happy that he received employment in his field, but I couldn't understand why God would take him away from our home even more than he had been in the past. Feeling frustrated, I cried to God one night and begged Him for understanding, asking that question "why." Falling asleep teary-eyed, I woke up with the answer, so clear in my mind. That gift of understanding and insight made a huge difference in my attitude and perseverance through the temporary situation.

Years later, I again asked God "why." I had a major car accident, and though I was protected from injury, I couldn't understand why God allowed it to happen. Later that day, He caused me to sit down and do my Bible study lesson which focused on the first chapter of Job. The study notes preceding that chapter plainly teach that we should not demand God to explain everything. God gives us Himself, not all the details of His plans. When we request insight and understanding and God decides it is best for us not to know, He gently tells us so. The timing of that study on that particular day was arranged by God.

"God alone knew the purpose behind Job's suffering, and yet he never explained it to Job. In spite of this, Job never gave up on God – even in the midst of suffering."[29] Job feared and trusted God. That is wisdom without having certain insight or knowledge. As Job "struggled to understand why all this was happening to him, it became clear that he was not meant to know the reasons. He would have to face life with the answers and explanations held back. Only then would his faith fully develop."[30]

Job never received an explanation for his misery or understood why he had to suffer through those devastating years. Yet, he clung to his faith and acknowledged God's sovereignty and wisdom in the end. And Job was richly rewarded.

Can we, like Job, trust God without answers and explanations for the heartaches in our lives? Can we remain faithful when we are tested? God chose to include Job's account in the Bible to teach us about perseverance and to encourage us. "For everything that was written in the past was written to teach us, so that through endurance and the encouragement of the Scriptures we might have hope" (Romans 15:4).

Solomon advised us to trust in the Lord with all of our heart (Proverbs 3:5). If we can trust God without reservation, we won't have any doubt or reluctance to obey Him, even when we are without understanding. Read Psalm 62:8 in the inset. Circle the words that tell us when we should trust God.

> "Trust in him at all times, O people; pour out your hearts to him, for God is our refuge."
> Psalm 62:8

When we trust the Lord, we are placing our confidence in Him and believing He is aware of our situation and is in control. We can be confident because the Bible reveals God's wisdom and power, along with His love for us. Because God is unchanging – He's the same yesterday as He is today and will be tomorrow[31] – we are assured that He still lovingly utilizes His wisdom and power on our behalf. We have to remember that ultimately, God has the big picture in mind. What life situation are you presently struggling with, in which you need to trust Him?

_____

Prayer For Today:

Thank God that He gives us wisdom when we ask for and seek it with the right motives.

Ask God for peace when you lack understanding and for His guidance as you trust Him.

_____

_____

_____

Day Three: Spiritual Wisdom

Do you consider yourself wise? _____ Do others consider you to be wise? _____

In our last lesson, we discussed Solomon and Job – examples of God giving and withholding understanding and insight. Solomon was the wisest person ever, but Job also had wisdom; both men were wise. Job was considered to be a man who "was blameless and upright; he feared God and shunned evil" (Job 1:1). How does Solomon define a wise man in Proverbs 14:16? Fill in the blanks.

"A _____ man _____ the Lord and

_____ _____, but a fool is hotheaded and reckless."

> **"Fear of the LORD is the foundation of true wisdom. All who obey his commandments will grow in wisdom."**
> **Psalm 111:10**

Read Psalm 111:10 (NLT) in the inset. The Hebrew word for "fear" in this verse means "reverence, a reverential trust in God that includes commitment to His word."[32] The fear of God and having reverential trust in Him is the beginning of wisdom. To grow in wisdom, we must obey God's words; obeying God brings spiritual insight into all of life. Is there a difference between worldly wisdom and spiritual wisdom? Yes! In 1st Corinthians 2:10-16 (NLT), Paul gave us a comparison:

> But it was to us that God revealed these things by his Spirit. For his Spirit searches out everything and shows us God's deep secrets. No one can know a person's thoughts except that person's own spirit, and no one can know God's thoughts except God's own Spirit. And we have received God's Spirit (not the world's spirit), so we can know the wonderful things God has freely given us. When we tell you these things, we do not use words that come from human wisdom. Instead, we speak words given to us by the Spirit, using the Spirit's words to explain spiritual truths. But people who aren't spiritual can't receive these truths from God's Spirit. It all sounds foolish to them and they can't understand it, for only those who are spiritual can understand what the Spirit means. Those who are spiritual can evaluate all things, but they themselves cannot be evaluated by others. For, "Who can know the Lord's thoughts? Who knows enough to teach him?" But we understand these things, for we have the mind of Christ.

The spirit of human wisdom apart from God is controlled by the physical and worldly life, a life without the Holy Spirit. That wisdom is available to everyone through investigation, research or experience. But such methods can tell us nothing about God's thoughts and plans. Worldly wisdom cannot understand spiritual wisdom. The difference between worldly wisdom and spiritual wisdom is the Holy Spirit, who has the mind of Christ and enters believers at their profession of faith. The Holy Spirit gives us understanding of spiritual things which influences the way we perceive the world.

> *The difference between worldly wisdom and spiritual wisdom is the Holy Spirit, who has the mind of Christ and enters believers at their profession of faith.*

Believers who are given spiritual wisdom see reality – the sunglasses are taken off and they see life as it really is, not a limited view. Our vision is no longer shaded, and because of the light's effect, we see much more, and have a deeper understanding of this world. This causes our perspective on life to change. When we see the world with "spiritual eyes," we have spiritual insight and possess spiritual wisdom. Spiritual wisdom enables believers to understand the gospel and how to respond to it - to fear the Lord and obey His commands. People who possess only worldly wisdom cannot see the light of Jesus Christ and are walking around in darkness. In John 8:12, what did Jesus call Himself? _____

What did He say would happen to those who follow Him?

_____

_____

John explained it this way:

> This is the message we have heard from him and declare to you: God is light; in him there is no darkness at all. If we claim to have fellowship with him yet walk in the darkness, we lie and do not live by the truth. But if we walk in the light, as he is in the light, we have fellowship with one another, and the blood of Jesus, his Son, purifies us from all sin. (1John 1:5-7)

Having spiritual wisdom enables us to walk in the light and understand eternal truths. According to Ephesians 5:8, how are we to live?

_____

_____

What does the fruit of the light represent? (Ephesians 5:9)

_____

_____

What do we need to know? (Ephesians 5:10)

_____

_____

What are we to avoid and expose? (Ephesians 5:11)

_____

_____

Ephesians 5:8-11 informs us that as children of light, our actions should reveal our faith. If we have spiritual wisdom, we will act on it. We are encouraged to be a light to others and allow them to see Jesus Christ in us. Jesus gave these instructions:

> You are the light of the world. A city on a hill cannot be hidden. Neither do people light a lamp and put it under a bowl. Instead they put it on its stand, and it gives light to everyone in the house. In the same way, let your light shine before men, that they may see your good deeds and praise your Father in heaven. (Matthew 5:14-16)

Reflecting Jesus Christ is a result of our spiritual wisdom. The Holy Spirit within us helps us view the world with spiritual eyes and creates the desire in us to be more like Christ. Imitating

Jesus' life is a result of one's new attitude from perceiving the world differently. When we try to obey Jesus, we are acting on our spiritual wisdom. Paul urged his readers to "Be imitators of God" (Ephesians 5:1).

How have you acted on the spiritual wisdom that you have received so far?

_____

Spiritual wisdom is much more beneficial than worldly wisdom. The Bible speaks positively of spiritual wisdom and negatively of worldly wisdom, with good reason. We know that this life on earth is temporary and our eternal life will be determined by how we respond to the revelation we receive on earth. Worldly wisdom is limited to this present temporary life while spiritual wisdom enables us to prepare for our future eternal life.

God gives generously to all who ask for His wisdom. If you have never asked Him for spiritual wisdom, do so today. And keep requesting it day after day, for the Holy Spirit will continue to supply it and guide you. And the more spiritual wisdom you have, the more you will trust God in your life.

Prayer For Today:

Thank God for giving His light to you and for opening your eyes to see the world spiritually.

Ask God to direct you to someone who is still walking in darkness – that you may be a light and show them the way.

_____

_____

_____

"Blessed are those who have learned to acclaim you, who walk in the light of your presence, O Lord" (Psalm 89:15). There are blessings that come with spiritual wisdom and we'll discuss those in the next lesson.

Day Four: Wisdom's Benefits

I always wanted to be smart. I wanted to be able to get straight A's in school without much effort. I wish I had a friend like King Solomon who could have given me all the answers to my questions. Solomon isn't here, but the One who gave Solomon his wisdom is.

Whom do you go to for advice? _____

Why did you choose those people? _____

_____

Does anyone come to you for advice? It would be a privilege to be a person who could always give good godly advice, (like Solomon). When someone has the gift of wisdom from God and uses it to glorify Him and to help others, that person will be given more opportunities to use his/her gift and serve the Lord.

Wisdom—both worldly and spiritual—is desirable. My children came to me for advice less often when they were teenagers, an age when godly direction is needed. Something is amiss with that scenario, unless they approached the Source of all wisdom. Thankfully, the stage when kids know everything and view their parents as brainless doesn't last forever. My kids began asking for my insight and opinions again after they moved out of my house.

Individuals usually desire spiritual wisdom before they receive it. And the spiritually wise go to God for help. Since He is the source of all wisdom and knowledge, He wants us to rely on Him.

I had a friend who taught this principle to me in college. Jane lived across the hallway from me and she was the girl I wanted to be. She was completing college in 3 years instead of 4 and had straight A's. She was talented in many areas and fun to be around. We were sitting at the same table doing our homework, and Jane peered at me as I struggled with my paper. She encouraged me to ask God for help and shared Philippians 4:13 (NASB), "For I can do everything through Christ, who gives me strength." She offered to pray with me and ask God to give me the ability to write that paper. And I experienced His power. I knew in my mind that God is able, but I didn't apply that knowledge to my life. I needed heart application of my biblical knowledge to trust God to help me. It is easy to say you trust in God, but it is harder to actually do it.

By sharing her faith, Jane helped me live that verse, and it opened a doorway for me in my personal relationship with Jesus Christ. Now I go to Him for everything. Whenever I need a Bible verse, He delivers. After asking for God's help, He has given me the location of where to look for my lost things – car keys, cell phone, and reading glasses.

How quickly do you ask the Lord for help? He wants you to depend on Him and develop an intimate relationship with Him. Having spiritual wisdom directs you to the One who can help you with your problems, even when they are trivial.

Besides being able to rely on God and His biblical truths, spiritual wisdom grants other benefits. Match the benefits of wisdom with these verses found in Proverbs 3:

Verse 2	safety
Verse 4	overflowing barns & vats filled with new wine
Verse 6	sweet sleep
Verse 8	prosperity and a prolonged life
Verse 10	no fear
Verse 23	our paths be straight
Verse 24	win favor and a good name
Verse 25	health to our body and nourishment to our bones

"Discretion will protect you, and understanding will guard you" (Proverbs 2:11). Discretion is the ability to tell right from wrong and enables the believer to detect evil motives in other people. This inner sense is developed by knowing and applying God's moral standards in our lives.

In the New Testament, Colossians 1:9-12 reveals that Paul and Timothy asked God to fill the believers in Colosse "with the knowledge of his [God's] will through all spiritual wisdom and understanding." This is so they:

> may live a life worthy of the Lord and may please him in every way:
> bearing fruit in every good work, growing in the knowledge of God,
> being strengthened with all power according to his glorious might so that
> you may have great endurance and patience, and joyfully giving thanks
> to the Father, who has qualified you to share in the inheritance of the
> saints in the kingdom of light.

How do we gain knowledge of God's will? One way is by reading what He revealed to us in the Bible. When we possess spiritual insight and understanding, we desire to submit to God's will. Why is it important to know and submit to His will?

_____

_____

_____

Paul advocated to get to know the Lord's will so we can live a life worthy of the Lord and please Him. Look at all the benefits of spiritual wisdom in the Colossians 1:9-12 passage:

"I keep asking that the God of our Lord Jesus Christ, the glorious Father, may give you the Spirit of wisdom and revelation, so that you may know him better." Ephesians 1:17

- Knowing God's will (leads to)
- Living a worthy life and pleasing God (so that)
- We can bear fruit - produce good works – (and)
- Continue to grow in knowledge of God.
- Be strengthened with God's power (so that we have)
- Great endurance,
- Patience, (and be)
- Joyful (for being qualified to)
- Share in the inheritance of the saints.

Read Ephesians 1:17 in the inset. Why did Paul ask God to give the believers in Ephesus the Spirit of wisdom and revelation?

Spiritual wisdom leads us to seek God - to know His will so we can live in obedience to Him, strengthened with His power, and please Him. The better we know God, the more we want to please and serve Him. This attitude elicits additional blessings as He reveals Himself to us even more, and the snowball effect deepens our trust in Him.

> *Spiritual wisdom leads us to seek God - to know His will so we can live in obedience to Him, strengthened with His power, and please Him.*

"We know also that the Son of God has come and has given us understanding, so that we may know him who is true" (1John 5:20).

Jane possessed spiritual wisdom, experienced those blessings, and trusted God long before I did. I thank God that she was a light and shared her spiritual wisdom with me. With whom can you share your spiritual wisdom?

_____ and _____

Look for the opportunities that arise and don't be afraid to show someone else how to walk in the light.

Prayer For Today:

Thank God for His gift of wisdom and all the benefits you receive for knowing His words and obeying them.

Ask God to give you spiritual wisdom with understanding and insight so you can know Him better.

_____

_____

_____

For additional study, read Psalm 112 and Proverbs 2, which reveal other blessings from having wisdom and fearing God.

Day Five: Be Wise

I remember being told when I was younger not to be a "smart aleck" or a "wiseacre." I usually received that comment after trying pick apart something my parent said. Yet, as reprimanding as that comment was intended to be, I wasn't offended at the insult. I rather liked the idea of being able to twist another person's words for a different meaning if it bettered my situation. I did that in fun, but it is frightening that many people do that today with the Bible.

In Colossians 1:10 (from the previous lesson), Paul asserted that bearing fruit (doing good things) and growing in the knowledge of God are outcomes of spiritual wisdom and understanding. In other words, to be wise is to act on our spiritual understanding which involves:

1) staying in God's Word and continuing to grow in the knowledge of God
2) bearing fruit in every good work.

Let's look at staying in God's Word first. In the Bible, the Lord gave guidelines on how to live our lives and how to have inner peace and joy. Whatever He said is as good as a promise. Since Jesus and His word are truth, it is guaranteed. But we have to read the Bible to know what these truths are. And then we can claim these promises through prayer. It is like having money in a bank that requires the owner's signature before it can be drawn out and used. If we don't make a withdrawal, the account is just a number and doesn't help anyone. Similarly, all of the Lord's beneficial principles are found in Scripture and are available for withdrawal, to be acted on.

What truths do you regularly claim and experience? The Lord is forever faithful to His words that are recorded in the Bible.

With biblical knowledge and discernment, we are better equipped to avoid being persuaded by false messages or temptations of sin.

Seekers gain knowledge, understanding and discernment (given by the Holy Spirit) when studying God's words. If we don't know His book, we are vulnerable to be led astray. A lot of people can proclaim messages from the Bible, but if we haven't personally read it and know what it says, we can't verify if another person's words are biblical or not. That is one reason why people join cults and believe lies. They don't know what the Bible actually says about the message they are hearing; meanwhile, what they hear sounds pretty good.

The Bereans went home and checked the Scriptures to see if Paul was preaching the truth (Acts 17:11). We should imitate the Bereans. With biblical knowledge and discernment, we are better equipped to avoid being persuaded by false messages or temptations of sin.

Has anyone ever convinced you of something that you later learned was untrue? People claim they've discovered new ways or "secrets" that help them live the best life possible, and they are trying to convince others to believe their message and buy their books. Be very discerning for everything you need to know is in the Bible. Quite often those "insights" are not biblical and are propelled by Satan. Discernment is also needed to detect when Scripture is taken out of context and given a twist in its meaning, or diluted to justify immoral behavior and excuse sin. Your spiritual wisdom grows by personally studying the Bible, which enables you to recognize false teachings.

Being spiritually wise is a process. Staying in communion with God and studying His Word is important because our world and our lives are constantly changing. Receiving godly direction avoids pitfalls and unnecessary difficulties. Our personal relationship with the Lord is healthy when it is steadily growing. How often are you in God's Word?_____

As you study Scripture, your personal relationship with the Lord will grow, along with your knowledge of who Jesus is and what He wants, and you will become more like Him. Do people see Jesus in you? Jesus possessed the fruit of the Holy Spirit which defined His character. Read Galatians 5:22-23 in the inset. How many attributes are listed? _____ Jesus' character affected the way He lived His life. You too, can bear fruit when you possess the Holy Spirit and ask Him to help you adopt a Christ-like disposition.

> "But the fruit of the Spirit is love, joy, peace, patience, kindness, goodness, faithfulness, gentleness and self-control."
> Galatians 5:22-23

Bearing fruit is our second point. Like a tree that bears or produces delicious fruit, godly lives produce spiritual fruit. Bearing fruit is the effect or consequence of one's godly attitude and actions; it's to be productive in doing good works that glorify God. Being fruitful is to have God's purposes and plans fulfilled through us. We read in Ephesians 2:10, "For we are Christ's workmanship, created in Christ Jesus to do good works, which God prepared in advance for us to do."

How do we become fruitful? We bear fruit when we allow God to work through us to bring Him glory. The Holy Spirit aids our choices in determining what to do with our lives. God gives us much freedom in those choices, and even helps us by giving us gifts and talents with which to serve Him. If you enjoy doing something, you are probably gifted or talented in that area. Do you have any special interests or hobbies? Are you willing to try new things? What do you like to do? _____

What do others say you are good at? _____

Think of different ways that you can be helpful to others by doing something you enjoy. Consider your church, community, neighbors, the elderly, sick or disabled. If you have difficulty coming up with ideas, ask God to show you. He will not only show you, but will also open the door for you with opportunities. We serve God wholeheartedly by serving others. What does Ephesians 6:7-8 add to that? _____

Jesus Christ did not come to earth to be served. What are the two reasons for His existence on earth, given in Mathew 20:28? _____

Jesus taught His disciples the lesson of serving others. Read John 13:12-17. What did He do? _____
Jesus exemplified that no man's importance or position on earth excuses him from serving others. After demonstrating the principle, He told His disciples they would be blessed if they followed His example and humbled themselves to serve others.

In John15:8, Jesus clarified, "This is *to my Father's glory*, that you bear much fruit, showing yourselves to be my disciples." When we serve God and others, we bear fruit. Spiritual fruit is Christ's character and personality developed and deployed in us.

Can others see fruit in your life? Is your fruit spiritual or spoiled?

Our motive and attitude in serving affects our fruit. "Each man should give what he has decided in his heart to give, not reluctantly or under compulsion, for God loves a cheerful giver" (2 Corinthians 9:7). Our attitude is more important to God than any possession we give or service we do. Jesus Christ wants us to serve Him and others willingly and cheerfully for His Father's glory. Our reason for bearing fruit is not for the service itself or for recognition, but to glorify (give honor and praise to) our God. Reread what Jesus said in John 15:8 (last page), and focus on the italicized words. Jesus glorified His Father in heaven. He publicly proclaimed, "Father, glorify your name!"[33] And later He prayed, "Glorify your Son, that your Son may glorify you."[34] David urged us to, "Glorify the Lord with me. Let us exalt his name together."[35]

What did Paul teach in Romans 15:6? Fill in the blanks.

"so that with one _____ and _____ you may

_____ the _____ and _____ of

our _____ Jesus Christ."

To be wise, we stay in God's Word and continually grow in our knowledge of Jesus Christ and in our personal relationship with Him. We try to be more like Him and glorify God our Father as we serve Him and others, and consequently bear fruit. This is living a life worthy of the Lord that brings eternal reward. This is trusting Him with our lives.

Prayer For Today:

Thank Jesus Christ for being the best example to imitate.

Ask God to help you find ways to serve Him and live a life worthy of the Lord.

_____

_____

_____

CHAPTER THREE DISCUSSION/REVIEW QUESTIONS

1. What thoughts come to mind when you acknowledge that God knows you better than you know yourself?

2. In what ways has God protected you or kept you (or a family member) safe?

3. Have you ever asked God for wisdom or insight? How did He respond?

4. In your own words, what is the difference between worldly wisdom and spiritual wisdom?

5. How do we remain faithful when we are tested?

6. Do you know anyone who seems to have been tested a lot lately? How can you encourage them?

7. How do you tend to look at the world – with sunglasses on or off?

8. Whom do you know that is still walking in darkness? How often have you prayed that God would cause your paths to cross so you can be used by Him as a light?

9. Whom or where do you go for advice? Why?

10. How quickly do you turn to God for help?
(small and insignificant things → life-threatening)

11. Why is it important to know God's will?

12. What godly principles do you live by and consequently experience God's faithfulness?

13. How easily are you persuaded by others? Do you believe everything your minister says from the pulpit? Have you ever questioned your pastor's message and examined its truth in the Bible?

14. Can others see fruit in your life? (Ask your Christian friends or family.)

15. How are you presently serving the Lord? If you're not, what would you like to do?

Chapter Four: God's Love

Day One: Biblical Descriptions and Assurances

> "And he passed in front of Moses, proclaiming, 'The Lord, the Lord, the compassionate and gracious God, slow to anger, abounding in love and faithfulness, maintaining love to thousands, and forgiving wickedness, rebellion and sin.'"
> Exodus 34:6-7

One of the first things young children learn in church is that God is love. Songs like *Jesus Loves Me* and *Jesus Loves the Little Children* are favorites of kids of all ages. A popular Bible verse often memorized is John 3:16, "For God so loved the world that he gave his one and only Son, that whoever believes in him shall not perish but have eternal life."

Why do you think God loves us? It's because of who He is - "God is love" - which the apostle John affirmed in 1John 4:8. God does not merely love others; He *is* love. Love is His nature, His character, and the expression of His being. Everything God does flows from His love.

Read Exodus 34:6-7 in the inset. How did God identify Himself to Moses?

_____

_____

_____

God's character is identified as compassionate, gracious, patient, faithful, forgiving, and loving. His love is defined by adjectives and adverbs that are repeated over and over in the Old Testament. What are the phrases that describe God's love in these verses?

Exodus 15:13; Psalm 107:8,15,21,31; _____

Psalm 86:5,15; Jonah 4:2 _____

1 Chronicles 16:34; Psalm 118:1-4,29 _____

How many times is the phrase "endures forever" mentioned in Psalm 136? _____

Many more verses in the Bible mention these descriptive words about God's love. Maybe with enough repetition, it might sink into our heads that God's love is unfailing, abounding, and endures forever. What do these three phrases mean? God's abounding love is great in amount and inexhaustible. He has a never-ending supply, and enough for everyone. His unfailing love means that it cannot err or fail; it's infallible, perfect, steadfast, and dependable. And God's love for us will never stop but continue forever; it's eternal. We cannot earn God's love and we cannot lose it.

Another children's song contains the lyrics, "I am so glad that my Father in heaven tells of His love in the book He has given. Wonderful things in the Bible I see – this is the dearest that Jesus loves me."[36]

Draw a line to match what the Bible says about God's love and where it is referenced.

Nothing can separate us from the love of God	Proverbs 3:12
God loves us so much that He calls us His children	John 15:9
Jesus loves us just as the Father loves Jesus	Romans 8:38-39
The Lord disciplines those He loves	Ephesians 3:18-19
Christ's love for us surpasses knowledge and fills us	1 John 3:1

David repeatedly wrote about the greatness of God's love in the Psalms. What do these verses mention about God's great love?

Psalm 57:10 _____

Psalm 103:11 _____

Psalm 103:17 _____

Just like His wisdom, God's love cannot be measured. The infinite span of His love is more than man's time. It is impossible to get beyond God's loving reach. Yet, many people have events or experiences in their lives that have caused them to think that God doesn't love them anymore. Have you ever felt this way? Write below what happened (or didn't happen) that made you (or someone you know) question whether God forgot about you or stopped loving you.

_____

_____

> There is nothing in this world that can separate us from God's love.

When times are tough, we sometimes feel like we have been abandoned by God. But if we never struggle, our faith would not grow or deepen. We must never let our doubts overwhelm us. David cried out to God when he wrote, "How long, O Lord? Will you forget me forever? How long will you hide your face from me?" (Psalm 13:1). And after David vented his feelings, the Lord calmed his soul, for the psalmist wrote just five sentences later, "But I trust in your unfailing love; my heart rejoices in your salvation" (verse 5).

Believers have always had to face hardships in many forms: illness, poverty, danger, injustice, and pain. Difficulties and heartaches may mislead us into thinking that God doesn't care anymore or no longer loves us; however, our thoughts and feelings are often wrong. Satan tries to make us think irrationally and he deceives believers into feeling alienated from God. The truth is, there is nothing in this world that can separate us from God's love.

When we don't trust God, our doubt or unbelief keeps us from being assured of His love. And without that assurance, we can't be comforted by His love. That's a sad situation because God never stops loving us and wanting the best for us. Our doubts cannot destroy God's love. It is like the child's game of Peek-a-Boo. You can put your hands over your eyes and pretend all you want, but the other person is still there. There may be obstacles in the way that block your vision, but that other person still sees you clearly. Likewise, we can totally convince ourselves that God quit loving us, but when we open our eyes, and the obstacles disappear, we see that His love never left us.

Fill in the blanks for Isaiah 54:10.

"Though the mountains be shaken and the hills be removed, yet

my _____ _____ for you will not be

_____..."

Romans 8:38-39 contains one of the most comforting promises in all of Scripture. Paul mentioned everything he could think of to help us grasp the concept that nothing can separate us from the love of God. Through Paul's letter, God assures us that His love is great and we can feel totally secure in Him. Fill in the blanks for Romans 8:38-39.

"For I am convinced that neither _____ nor life, neither

angels nor _____, neither the _____

nor the _____, nor any _____, neither

_____ nor _____, nor _____

else in all creation, will be able to _____ us from the

_____ of God that is in Christ Jesus our Lord."

Every individual who personally knows God enjoys a certainty of His great love. This divine love will never be weakened or changed. In the universe, God's love is the strongest, steadiest, firmest, most constant and dependable love of all. It's hard to comprehend because our love is not perfect like His. We love conditionally; it is dependent upon the circumstances. But God's love is unconditional and is called "agape" love. Basically, it's an unmerited, self-giving love. Agape is neither a love for the deserving nor a love that desires to possess, but it seeks to give.

Jesus was the greatest expression of love that ever came into the world. While it is not recorded that He ever told one person the words, "I love you," Jesus did refer to His love for others while teaching. According to John 13:34, Jesus was training His disciples when He said, "As I have loved you, so you must love one another."

People knew that Jesus loved individuals. John is referred to as "the disciple whom Jesus loved."[37] John 11:5 states, "Jesus loved Martha and her sister and Lazarus." Mary and Martha sent word to Jesus that "the one you love is sick."[38] After Jesus saw Mary weeping, He wept, and the Jews commented, "See how he loved him!"[39] Jesus did not love with just words, but with actions and in truth.[40] He healed the sick, fed the hungry, befriended and helped the outcasts, and forgave sinners.

It has been reported that 85% of all love is non-verbal. If your actions contradict your words, what are people going to believe - your words or your actions? Your actions, of course, because actions speak louder than words. One will walk their talk, (their actions will be consistent with their words), if they are sincere.

God's love is displayed most clearly at the cross where Christ suffered and died for us, while we were dead from our sins (Ephesians 2:1). The beneficiaries of agape love never do anything to merit it; lucky us, we are the undeserving recipients upon whom the Lord lavishes that love. Get used to it, we are dearly loved by Him.[41]

Prayer For Today:

Thank God that He loves you unconditionally.

Ask God for the confidence to never doubt His love again.

_____

_____

_____

Day Two: Biblical Evidences of God's Love

Have you ever questioned whether someone really loved you? It could be their tone of voice when telling you or the way they treat you that makes you doubt. How wonderful it is to have an all-knowing God who loves you unconditionally!

Throughout Scripture, much evidence is given of God's love. Besides the apostles writing about it, we perceive from Jesus' life that He is the essence of love. His compassion for people was second to none. All the miracles Jesus performed to heal and feed were freely given as a result of His love. His reaching out to the "undesirables" (those who were hated or considered unclean) was unmatched. His life was a living illustration of how to love others.

The most convincing evidence of God's love for us is giving His Son to die for our sins. Read 1John 4:9-10 in the inset. What does this passage tell us about how God showed

> "This is how God showed his love among us: He sent his one and only Son into the world that we might live through him. This is love: not that we loved God, but that he loved us and sent his Son as an atoning sacrifice for our sins."
> 1 John 4:9-10

His love? _____

_____

What do you think is an atoning sacrifice? _____

_____

To atone for something means to make a satisfactory action for an offense which will then produce reconciliation (the restoration of a relationship). When man sinned, the consequence of that sin was death. So it meant the shedding of blood (death) became necessary to atone for everyone's sins. The blood of the sacrificed animals was the provisional atonement, but it could not fully satisfy the penalty of man's sin. Repeatedly sacrificing animals was the temporary way to deal with repeated sin until Jesus' death occurred. Jesus Christ sacrificed Himself and replaced all sacrifices; His was the one that would once and for all atone for man's sin.[42] Remember that only someone perfect, without sin, could take the place of the sinner; Jesus Christ was the only sinless person who ever lived. "For Christ died for sins once for all, the righteous for the unrighteous, to bring you to God" (1Peter 3:18). So as Jesus willingly died on the cross when He did no wrong, He took the punishment of our sin for us (death with separation from God). Fill in the blanks of 1John 2:2.

"He is the _____ _____ for

our _____, and not only for _____ but also for the sins

of the _____ _____."

Jesus paid the penalty of man's sin. Then He arose the third day and later ascended into heaven. Likewise, God will raise us up and give us the privilege of spending eternity with Him in a perfect relationship. But first we must believe that Jesus is our Lord God and Savior.

In Luke 1:35, we read that an angel told Mary that the Holy Spirit would come upon her and she would conceive and give birth to the Holy One who was to be called the Son of God. He was totally man and totally God because He was born of Mary and the Holy Spirit.

John 1:1,14 reveals that in the beginning was the Word and the Word was God. The Word became flesh and made His dwelling among us.

Paul declared that Christ is God over all.[43] What is written about Jesus Christ in Colossians 2:9?

_____

_____

The fact that Jesus is God is the reason His life on earth was without depravity. His being human was the reason He suffered and was tested (but chose not to sin). Jesus' humanity allowed Him to experience everything we experience – rejection, injustice, pain, sorrow, and the list goes on. From the following passages, what emotions did Jesus, because of His humanity, experience?

Mark 6:34 _____   Luke 22:44 _____

Mark 14:33-34 _____   John 11:5, 35 _____

Luke 7:9 _____   John 13:21 _____

Luke 10:21 _____   Hebrews 13:12 _____

Read 2 Peter 1:1 in the inset. What title did Peter give Jesus?

_____

Therefore, we can conclude that Jesus Christ, both fully human and divine, is our God and Savior. Our salvation is based upon the acknowledgment that we are sinful and deserve death,[44] and that Jesus Christ is the One who died in our place and took the punishment for our sins. No other being could be our substitute.

> "...To those who through the righteousness of our God and Savior Jesus Christ have received a faith as precious as ours..."
> 2 Peter 1:1

Jesus' death bridged the gap between God and us, which originated with the first sin. At Jesus' death, the thick temple curtain (that separated sinful people from the Most Holy Place representing God's presence) was torn from the top to the bottom by God.[45] This symbolized that sin's penalty of death was now paid, our sins are forgiven, and nothing separates us from God anymore. Jesus is the One through whom we can come to God our Father. His life and death saved us from our sins and enabled us to have a restored relationship with God that will continue after our bodies die. Faith in Jesus Christ as our Savior gives us eternal life with Him and the Father. What did Jesus say about Himself in John 14:6?

_____

Jesus is not one of the ways we get to heaven, He is the only way.

Jesus is not one of the ways we get to heaven, He is the only way. In the early church, Christianity was sometimes called "the Way" (Acts 9:2; 19:9,23). Fill in the blanks to complete Romans 5:8.

"But God _____ his own _____ for us in this: While we were still _____, Christ _____ for _____."

If God loved us despite our sinfulness, (when we're totally unworthy), and sent His Son to die for sinners, how much He must love us now as His adopted children who have faith in His Son, Jesus. What reason did the angel give Joseph for Jesus to be born of Mary and the Holy Spirit? Find your answer in Matthew 1:21.

According to Luke 19:10, for what purpose did Jesus say He came to earth?

_____

The name Jesus means "the Lord saves." Jesus came to earth to save us because we can't save ourselves from sin and its consequences. No matter how good we are, we can't eliminate the sinful nature that is present in all of us. Jesus didn't come to earth to help people save themselves. He came to be their Savior from the power and penalty of sin. We cannot earn our salvation; it is a gift from God. No matter how good we are, we will always fall short of perfection. Ephesians 2:8-9 reinforces this concept. Read it in the inset. How have we been saved?

_____

_____

"For it is by grace you have been saved, through faith – and this not from yourselves, it is the gift of God – not by works, so that no one can boast."
Ephesians 2:8-9

We may not "feel" saved when we sin, but thank God, our salvation is not dependent on our feelings. Fill in the blanks for Romans 10:9.

"That if you _____ with your

_____, '_____ is

_____,' and _____ in your

_____ that God _____

him from the _____, you will be

_____."

Another childhood song gives the simple message,

> For God so loved the world, He gave His only Son, to die on Calvary's tree, from sin to set me free. Some day He's coming back – what glory that will be! Wonderful His love to me.[46]

Prayer For Today:

Thank God that He loved us so much that He sent Jesus to take the punishment of our sin.

Ask God to bring to mind your sins so you may confess them, ask for forgiveness, and repent. Then ask Him to allow you to experience His love and comfort that only He can give.

_____

_____

_____

Day Three: Personalize God's Love

It is easy to say phrases like "God is love" and "God loves you." But how often do we say to ourselves, "God loves me?" Do we live our lives in such a way that demonstrate we believe it? God loves us despite our bad moods, attitudes, and actions. Nothing we do will cause God to stop loving us because His love is based on who He is, not on what we've done. This is hard to accept because we live in a performance-driven culture where everything is earned.

David proclaimed, "For great is your love toward me" (Psalm 86:13). He personalized God's love and lived his life with that in mind. Believing in that love enabled him to trust God. Experiencing God's love was so special that David had to write about it. When we feel the Lord's amazing love, we want to tell others.

Read the following paragraph and fill every blank with the word "me" as you read it.

God knows _____ better than I know myself. And He still loves _____, cherishes _____, cares for _____, and wants to have a deeper, loving relationship with _____. God will never stop loving _____, even if my emotions fool me into thinking that He has. He loves _____ not for what I do or don't do, (because my actions cannot earn His love), but He loves _____ for who I am in Christ Jesus.

Textbook knowledge about God's love is different from experiencing it. Like many people, I had unrealistic expectations of marriage. I thought my husband and I would have this blissful love relationship and be able to witness to others how great a Christian marriage could be. God must have chuckled with that one. The truth is we fought on our honeymoon. Our expectations of each other were unmet and I walked around with a big hole in my heart for years. I wanted to feel more loved. I longed for a tension-free relationship filled with total loving acceptance and respect. The awareness of how things should be made the reality of how things were all the more disappointing. I looked for that hole to be filled at home, work, and church, always striving to be the best. Obviously, I had the wrong strategy. Even with years of biblical education, I did not understand that God wanted me to turn to Him. I foolishly thought that since He allowed me to have marital problems right after the wedding, He wasn't going to solve them. So I had to deal with them by myself. I chose to search for a balance in my life – to find joy and fulfillment in other things. My parents, friends, co-workers, and every relationship would fall short of filling that emptiness. Eventually, I developed an ache in my soul that sought relief.

Nineteen years later, God led me to a community Bible study which took my head knowledge and helped me apply it to my heart. And He caused me to realize that my empty feeling—the hole in my heart—was given to me by Him, to be filled only by Him. God created humans with a need for His love and to have a personal relationship with Him.

I knew that God loved everyone and wanted a relationship with us, but I thought my belief in Him and my service in the church was the relationship. However, it wasn't personal enough and that's why I didn't feel His love. That is, until I realized how wrong I had been trying to be independent. I poured my heart out to the Lord, asked for forgiveness, and recommitted my life to Him. And the love I had been craving for so long came flooding into my soul.

During all those years, God wanted all of me, my undivided time, my love, my problems and cares – basically, my heart. He desires an intimate relationship that communicates with Him daily. This relationship, which developed quickly, filled me and surprisingly produced joy. Experiencing God's love and joy was so satisfying that I quit aching inside, and instead, felt this wonderful inner peace. When we make Jesus Christ number one in our lives, then other relationships are viewed in the right perspective with the proper expectations. Jesus is the ultimate fulfillment of our needs.

> *When we realize that Jesus knows us completely and loves us for who we are, we understand the depth of His love for us as sinners.*

Furthermore, I believe there are many lonely people who sit in our churches and are searching to fill their own emptiness. Admitting your feelings and sinfulness to God and offering your heart and life to Him are the primary steps of submission. And He takes over from there, filling you with His love and peace. This enables your personal relationship with the Lord (that He deeply desires) to grow.

When we realize that Jesus knows us completely and loves us for who we are, we understand the depth of His love for us as sinners. We don't have to pretend or hope to be somebody that Jesus will eventually love.

Read Ephesians 3:17b-19 in the inset. What did Paul want us to grasp or understand?

_____

_____

Why? _____

Is experiencing God's love a one-time shot or can we continually feel His love? We get a taste of it when we confess our wrongdoings to Him and (re)commit our lives to Him. But that is only the beginning. The relationship the Lord desires to have with us gives back to us more than we could ever hope for. He continually quenches our hunger and thirst, and it tastes so good. He fills us up to the point where our cup overflows. Fill in the blanks to complete Psalm 107:8-9.

"Let them give thanks to the Lord for his

_____ _____ and his

wonderful _____ for men, for he

_____ the _____

and _____ the _____ with

_____ things."

"And I pray that you, being rooted and established in love, may have power, together with all the saints, to grasp how wide and long and high and deep is the love of Christ, and to know this love that surpasses knowledge – that you may be filled to the measure of all the fullness of God." Ephesians 3:17b-19

Jesus declared that He is the bread of life and is able to quench our hunger and thirst. From John 6:35, what must we do to never be hungry and thirsty again? _____

_____

Our relationships on earth will always fail us in some way. But God's love is unfailing. All we have to do is open our hearts to Him and experience it for ourselves.

How connected are you to the Lord? Do you feel His presence with you? Do you love Him? Put an X on the line that best describes your relationship with Him.

_____

Intimate   Very close   somewhat   occasional   what relationship?

Our Father in heaven wants to fill that hole or empty feeling, and invites us to know Him intimately and spend undivided time with Him. I've heard stories from people that have been declared dead but came back to life. All of those people who claimed they experienced heaven expressed similar feelings—the love they felt was indescribable. It was so wonderful, they didn't want to leave. What they felt just being in Jesus' presence without seeing Him was better than anything they ever felt on earth. That makes me realize how much I have missed by not coming into His presence more often through prayer.

If God understands us, loves and forgives us, and gives us peace and joy, why do we spend so little time and effort communicating with Him? If anyone on earth made us feel that good, we'd always want to be in their presence. We feel God's presence most frequently in prayer. Prayer is simply talking to God.

How would you describe your prayer life? Check what applies or write your own description.

       ☐ God's calling me, but I've been avoiding Him.

       ☐ God calls and gets my busy signal.

       ☐ I'm leaving a lot of messages but not getting any return calls.

       ☐ I talk a lot. God listens.

       ☐ We have great conversations.

       ☐ What's God's number again?

       ☐ _____

Do you talk to God only in emergency situations? Have you ever had a friend who called you only when he/she wanted something? After a while, you question whether the two of you have a real friendship or if the person is just taking advantage of your generosity. God wants to have conversations with you like a loving father would have with his son or daughter. Do you ever discuss what is happening in your life with Him? Or do you think that He already knows and telling Him would be wasted breath? It's true that God already knows what is on our minds; however, He still wants us to speak to Him because it's the relationship that He's after.

We may be faithful with our prayers and talking to God, but how effective are we at listening? It is an awesome experience to realize that God is speaking to you personally. Are you attentive enough to realize when He is talking to you? Do you hear Him?

It's easy to ignore sounds and conversation. Many students study with the radio on. Others go to sleep with music playing or a sound machine. Some people keep the television on all day. Spouses have selective hearing and parents tune out their children's chatter. I heard of a little boy who wanted to get his mother's complete attention. So he pulled her face toward his and asked her to listen to him with her eyes. Think about that. How do you listen to God?

_____

Listening to God means hearing followed by obeying, to understand in our hearts and respond with our attitudes and actions. Do we hear and obey? God gives many conditional promises to us, but we have to do what He says to activate them. When we strive to obey God, when we spend time with Him in prayer and listen to Him, when we enter His presence, He rewards us.

God's love is personal. And the best part of His love is that it feels so good. Without it, we sense something is missing in our lives and subconsciously search to fill the emptiness with other pleasures like food, shopping, sports, or friends. Instead of looking around, we need to look up. Temporary pleasure is no match for the joy of His love. Do you believe that God loves you? _____ How much do you love Him? _____

Prayer For Today:

Thank God for His immeasurable love.

Ask God to clear your schedule so you can spend uninterrupted time with Him. Time where your heart and mind can concentrate without distractions. Enough time so you can feel His love and quench your hunger or thirst.

_____

_____

_____

Day Four: Our Response

So God loves me. Now what? What does He want of me? In Matthew 22:34-40, we read that the Pharisees asked Jesus which was the greatest commandment in the Law. What was His reply?

_____

_____

How can you love God with all of your heart? All of your soul? All of your mind?

_____

_____

How do we please God? We can find out what He wants from us in the Scriptures. Draw a line to match the following verses with God's will for our lives.

Trust Him	Exodus 20:12
Honor father & mother	Luke 17:4
Believe His words	John 14:1
Pray for each other	John 14:11
Use our gifts to serve	John 14:15
Forgive others	Ephesians 6:18
Offer hospitality	1 Thessalonians 5:11
Encourage others	1 Peter 4:9
Obey Him	1 Peter 4:10

God gave the Ten Commandments to His children as part of His covenant. Obedience to His commands would bring Israel blessings, and breaking the covenant with intentional disobedience would bring punishment. Centuries later, Jesus summarized those laws into two parts. The first five commandments represent love to God while the last five show love to our neighbors. What other New Testament book (besides Matthew 22) records these two greatest commands given by Jesus? _____

What additional phrase about how to love the Lord is given in Mark 12? _____

Jesus combined the commandments from Deuteronomy 6:5 and Leviticus 19:18 to show that love for our neighbor is an outcome of love for God. But who is our neighbor? An expert in the law asked Jesus this question after quoting His summary about loving God and our neighbors. The Lord responded with a parable to illustrate what it means to love a neighbor. According to Luke 10:30-37, who is our neighbor?

_____

Jesus told this parable (an earthly story with a heavenly meaning) to someone who was supposed to know and understand the law. But the man needed insight for its application. Jesus used this story as an example of what real love involves. Love is shown as a sacrifice for the sake of others, even for those who may hate us, as the Jews felt about the Samaritans. Our neighbor is not necessarily one who lives in close proximity to us, but anyone we meet. Sacrificial love is not based on a feeling, but a determined act of the will, a resolve to put the welfare of others above our own. This agape love does not come naturally to humans. Because of our fallen nature, agape love can only come from God.

This is the love which has been poured out into our hearts through the Holy Spirit, whom God has given to us when we became His children.[47] When that love is in our hearts, we can obey Jesus who said, "A new command I give you: Love one another. As I have loved you, so you must love one another" (John 13:34). This new commandment involves loving one another as He loved us—sacrificially—even to the point of death. "This is how we know what love is: Jesus Christ laid down his life for us. And we ought to lay down our lives for our brothers" (1John 3:16). Because of God's love for us, we are able to love one another. And Paul urged believers to do just that. Fill in the blanks to complete Ephesians 5:1-2.

"Be _____ of God, therefore, as _____

_____ children and live a life of _____,

just as _____ _____ us and _____

_____ up for us as a fragrant _____ and

_____ to God."

Why should we love the people who hate us or persecute us? What did Jesus tell us to do concerning our enemies? Fill in the blanks for Matthew 5:44.

"But I tell you: _____ your _____ and

_____ for those who _____ you."

> "If anyone has material possessions and sees his brother in need but has no pity on him, how can the love of God be in him? Dear children, let us not love with words or tongue but with actions and in truth."
> 1 John 3:17-18

Jesus knew Judas Iscariot's evil heart but still humbled Himself to wash His betrayer's feet along with the other disciples' feet. Jesus instructed His followers to love their enemies because loving those who love us does not merit a reward. Even unbelievers do that.[48]

Is there anyone whom you dislike and avoid? Anyone who has hurt you or treated you unjustly? How about someone who just irritates you and brings out the worst in you? Pray for them. Pray that the Lord will soften their heart and help you to respond to them in a manner that will honor God. Ask the Holy Spirit to help you rise above your feelings and make the effort to love that person. Pray for peace, kindness, and unity among those with whom you feel friction.

Loving others with our actions is a theme that Jesus discussed with His disciples. He claimed that our deeds - stirred by our love with no thought of payback or benefit to self - are rewarded. What does Matthew 25:34-46 have in common with 1John 3:17-18 (printed in the inset)?

_____

_____

Jesus taught about our future judgment using a parable with sheep and goats, recorded in Matthew 25:31-46. He informed us that the rewards for loving others are not of this world. From verse 46, what happens to those who never helped their neighbor in need?

_____

What happens to those who helped others out of love? _____

Jesus' disciples understood this teaching, for they wrote letters to others about putting their love into action. John advocated the principle of loving God by loving others (1John 3:17-18). Read this Scripture passage again (in the last inset) and circle the words which express how God wants us to love. James also commented on serving others:

> What good is it, my brothers, if a man claims to have faith but has no deeds? Can such faith save him? Suppose a brother or sister is without clothes and daily food. If one of you says to him, "Go, I wish you well; keep warm and well fed," but does nothing about his physical needs, what good is it? In the same way, faith by itself, if it is not accompanied by action, is dead. (James 2:14-17)

A sincere love for God and others is accompanied by selfless actions and indicates an active faith.

A sincere love for God and others is accompanied by selfless actions and indicates an active faith. When we experience God's love in our hearts, gratitude materializes and causes a response. We not only love God in return, we want to do more and share God's love with others. This can take many different forms, but the end result is action - doing good deeds or serving others - in appreciation of our salvation. Our actions are a result of our faith. They do not earn our salvation but they emerge from our gratitude for already being saved.

Perhaps you are thinking of some people who are good, generous, law-abiding citizens who help others. But they have no desire to know what is written in the Bible and they live without a personal relationship with the Lord. They are saved too, right? Wrong.

There are many nice people in the world who do good things, but good works do not save us. Everyone has sinned and is accountable to God for that sin. It is belief and acceptance of Jesus Christ's atoning sacrifice that saves.

Understanding the gift of salvation motivates believers to gratefully respond to God's love. Belief in God without a commitment is no better than the demons, for they also believe in God and know that He exists and rules. Those angels ignore or reject God's love and purpose. But if our faith is sincere, we will love Jesus back, make Him our Lord, and want to obey all that He has commanded. The thankfulness in our hearts for His selfless, sacrificial love will be energetic.

When you follow Jesus' commands by loving Him and your neighbor as yourself, He rewards you beyond measure. When you put Jesus first, others second, and yourself last, what do you experience? _____ Look at the first letters of: Jesus, others, and yourself for your answer. Read John 15:10-11 in the inset.

> "If you obey my commands, you will remain in my love, just as I have obeyed my Father's commands and remain in his love. I have told you this so that my joy may be in you and that your joy may be complete."
> John 15:10-11

What will happen if we obey Jesus' commands?

_____

_____

Why did Jesus tell us this?

_____

_____

Prayer For Today:

Thank Jesus for His perfect, sacrificial love.

Ask the Holy Spirit to fill you with God's agape love so you can love others as Jesus does.

_____

_____

_____

Day Five: Second Chances

I love second chance drawings. (Those are when the winner is not present and another name or number is drawn.) I never win them but it gives me hope for a few more seconds. Not by chance, we always win when we hope in the Lord. Why? Because He's trustworthy! He proved it to us in the past with His life, death, and resurrection, and now God continues to love us and prepare us for eternal life with Him. This gift of love and salvation should produce immense gratitude in us and a desire to give back to God. How do we give back and show our appreciation? By submitting to His will and serving Him—doing what He tells us to do in the Bible. However, as we live for God, we realize how often we fall short, disobey Him, and continually need His forgiveness. The more like Jesus we become, the more conscious we are of our sins.

I am so grateful for God's forgiveness. There was a time when I thought I really blew it. I knew it was wrong, but because I didn't trust God to handle the situation, I did it my own way. I not only felt remorse afterwards, I thought I disappointed God so greatly that He wouldn't love me as much and would no longer use me or allow me to be His "good and faithful servant." I frantically tried to think of biblical events where someone willfully sinned and God forgave him and continued to use him. But I could only think of stories with negative endings that were a consequence to the sin. As I sobbed in my pillow, I begged God to forgive me and let me still serve Him. I searched the Bible for some encouragement. And then I found it: the parable of the prodigal son. That boy really screwed up, but realized his mistake and came back humbly to his father, who was waiting for his return. This godly father was joyful and restored the repentant son to his past position.

Even though that story encouraged me, I still feared that God wouldn't do the same for me. After all, it didn't really happen; it was a parable. I needed confirmation so I asked God that if He really did forgive me, love me, and would still use me, to please let me hear someone, anyone, say "prodigal son" in any type of conversation that day. It was a Sunday morning, so I didn't care if it was in the church service, in Sunday school, or overhearing someone else's conversation; I wanted to hear those words. It could even be on TV at night but I wanted desperately to audibly hear those words so I could be assured that it wasn't too late for me. I can't describe the deepness of that desire, but it permeated my soul. Sitting in the church pew, I anxiously looked at the title of the sermon in the bulletin, and it was a Christmas song. "No chance there," I thought, "I'd have to wait until Sunday school afterwards." So I asked God to help me concentrate on the sermon and learn from it. Two-thirds of the way into the message, the pastor actually said, "the parable of the prodigal son." Not only did he mention those words, he went on and talked about God's love and forgiveness for another minute. My heart pounded so hard, I thought my clothes would flap. With tears seeping from my eyes, I was filled with joy and relief. God convinced me that He still loved me, and He even provided the very confirmation I asked for. His love and mercy are truly amazing.

Sadly, many of us feel disqualified from serving God because of our past sins, especially when we repeat the same ones over and over again. Besides feeling like a failure, we think God considers us undeserving and will no longer use or bless us. Our peace becomes lost in our discouragement. However, when we read Scripture and learn that God gives second chances, we sense hope.

Have you ever felt that God would no longer want to use you because of your past mistakes? Feelings can be wrong. God uses the most unlikely people—all sinful—to serve His purposes. Which imperfect people did God still use to accomplish His plans? Read the verses, scan the chapters, and write the names on the lines provided.

_____ Exodus 2:11-15, 3

_____ Joshua 6:25

_____ Jonah 1-3

_____ Matthew 26:69-75; Acts 1-5, 9-12

_____ Acts 9, 13-28

Let's study these examples. Moses killed an Egyptian and fled to Midian. He ran away and became a shepherd. Yet, God chose to use him to lead the Israelites out of Egypt and through the wilderness to their new land of Canaan. He experienced many spectacular miracles, received the law from God, talked to Him face to face in the tent of meeting, and even saw God's glory.

A prostitute named Rahab heard about the God of Israel and feared Him. She acted on her belief and hid Israel's spies. Consequently, she and her family were spared from death when Israel defeated Jericho. This once sexually immoral lady eventually became an ancestor of David and Jesus.

Fleeing from his assignment, the prophet Jonah ended up inside a great fish. God gave him a second chance to deliver the message by causing the fish to vomit Jonah out on dry land. That message he finally gave caused a nation to repent, avoid destruction, and also receive a second chance.

Peter was part of Jesus' inner circle who knew Him intimately. Peter denied knowing Jesus not once or twice, but three times after insisting he would die with Jesus before he would disown Him. Peter had to feel sick to his stomach after meeting Jesus' eyes after that third denial. The Lord still loved Peter, forgave him, and used him to be an influential missionary and leader of the church. God gave Peter many more opportunities to stand up courageously and preach the gospel boldly.

> **"If we confess our sins, he is faithful and just and will forgive us our sins and purify us from all unrighteousness."**
> **1 John 1:9**

Saul, the Pharisee, used to hunt Christians. He persecuted and imprisoned them prior to his encounter with God and dramatic conversion. He later became the apostle Paul who claimed to be the most unworthy of all sinners. Yet, God chose him to be a missionary to the Gentiles and an author of many New Testament books in the Bible. His life had an enormous impact on the growth of Christianity.

The Bible records these events to teach us about our loving God. There is no one perfect, no one without sin. But God is merciful and forgives us. We must forgive ourselves for our past blunders because Jesus paid the price for them with His blood. If God forgives us when we repent, we must also forgive ourselves and move forward. When we repent, God erases our sins as though they never happened. Read 1John 1:9 in the inset. How does God react if we confess our sins? _____

_____

God doesn't keep a record of our wrongs, so we must not dwell on them. We may have temporary consequences to them, but Jesus changed the eternal consequences for us. He made it possible for repentant believers to move on, so we need to look forward instead of backwards.

On the other hand, Satan loves to make us focus on our faults and feel inadequate. He deceives us into believing we are unworthy by bringing back to mind all of our wrong turns and mistakes. He makes us feel like a failure. Satan causes us to doubt God's goodness and forgiveness, and steals our hope.

Like the examples given earlier, we too, can still be useful to God for He will provide us with opportunities to serve Him. God often takes our past failures and uses them for our good and to benefit others. We can be empathetic to others who experience

> *God often takes our past failures and uses them for our good and to benefit others.*

the same situations and help them through their difficult times. God will use whatever experiences we've had to fulfill His plans in serving Him.

The Lord loves us, never fails us, and always forgives us – even repeat offenders. His supply of compassion and grace is inexhaustible. His unending mercy is proven by the additional chances He continually gives us. What event(s) in your life can you use to encourage other people in their faith?

_____

How willing are you to give other people second chances? Consider also those people whose mistakes affected you personally.

_____

_____

What did Jesus say about forgiveness in these verses?

Colossians 3:13 _____

Mark 11:25 _____

Matthew 6:14-15 _____

Jesus revealed what will happen to us if we don't forgive others. Read the parable in Matthew 18:21-35. From verses 34-35, what did Jesus say will happen?

_____

_____

Jesus advised us to ask our Father in heaven for forgiveness and for help in forgiving others. This is recorded in Luke 11:4, where Jesus spoke the Lord's Prayer and said, "Forgive us our sins for we also forgive everyone who sins against us." Just as we receive forgiveness and second chances from our Lord, so we must also love others and do the same for them.

Prayer For Today:

Thank God that when you repent, He forgives and forgets your sin, and continues to use you.

Ask God to reveal how your past and present can be used to benefit others and make a difference for Him.

_____

_____

_____

CHAPTER FOUR DISCUSSION/REVIEW QUESTIONS

1. Why does God love us and want a personal relationship with us?

2. When did you first realize that God loves you?

3. How would you convince a child or friend that God loves him/her?

4. How is Jesus both fully God and fully man?

5. Why did Jesus become an atoning sacrifice?

6. How do you respond to those who say there are different ways that people can get to heaven?

7. How often do you talk with the Lord? How well do you listen to Him?

8. What distractions keep you from praying? How do you keep your mind from wandering when you pray?

9. Are you comfortable leading group prayer? If not, why not? How does one ever reach that comfort level?

10. Who is our neighbor? How can we begin to love those whom we dislike?

11. Why is it important to obey God by loving others?

12. Is forgiving yourself easy or difficult?

13. Is serving God an earned position? (In the parable of the talents, why were the "good and faithful" servants given more?)

14. How willing are you to give other people second chances? Does it make it harder when their offense was directly against you or your children?

15. Why should we forgive others?

Chapter Five: Troubles and Tears

Day One: Biblical Troubles

Life is not fair! Nor is it easy. All of us face adversity in various forms and at different times. The Bible records stories of godly people who experienced much trouble and many tears. But trusting God helped them through their difficult situations. Give the <u>names</u> of the people who suffered and the <u>reason</u> for their troubles and tears from the references given.

Genesis 39:20; _____
      40:15

1 Samuel 1:6-7 _____

1 Samuel 19:10-11; _____
      20:41

2 Kings 20:1-3 _____

Job 1:13-20; _____
    2:7-9

Daniel 3:16-21 _____

Luke 22:61-62 _____
Acts 5:40; 12:1-5

2 Corinthians 11:24-28 _____

Matthew 26:37-39; _____
      27:26-31

Sometimes when we read about other people's problems, we tend to gloss over the words without visualizing the pain or fear they endured. Reading sentences doesn't always portray the full extent of the suffering involved. But these events really happened and produced heart-wrenching emotion.

Let's look at Joseph's life. He was thrown into a pit by his jealous brothers who hated him, and then sold into slavery, separating him from his loving father for 22 years. He was falsely accused by Potiphar's wife and sent to prison. He pleaded (not just a casual chat) with Pharoah's cupbearer to "get me out of this prison" (Genesis 40:14). Joseph was desperate and asked for help from humans besides trusting God.

Hannah wanted children. It was bad enough being barren and sharing her husband with another woman, but that woman provoked and irritated her to the point of tears and no appetite. Being taunted for the very reason of the sorrow in your heart is cruel. Hannah turned to the Lord in her misery, and prayed because of her "great anguish and grief" (1 Samuel 1:16).

David found himself on the run. Saul was jealous and repeatedly tried to kill him. He had to say goodbye to his best friend, Jonathan, forever; "David wept the most" (1 Samuel 20:41). And for the next 13 years, David had to hide, flee, live in caves and fields, and fight his enemies while waiting for God to fulfill his anointing as king. It was a dangerous and unpleasant time living as a fugitive; yet, He trusted God's timing.

Hezekiah was ill and received his death notice. Throughout his life, he consciously tried to obey God, and he did not want to die yet. He "wept bitterly" (2 Kings 20:3). Knowing you are going to die soon produces a range of emotions. Thankfully, the story didn't end with his bitter tears. Hezekiah prayed for himself because he knew that the Lord finds favor with those who faithfully seek to serve Him. His hope was based on his life's trust in God.

Job is known for persevering through his hardships that God allowed, without ever knowing the reason why. Losing all his livestock, servants, and children wasn't enough. Satan wanted him to be in pain with sores over his entire body. Furthermore, his support group failed him and even his wife encouraged him to curse God and die. Talk about misery! After Job prayed for his friends (whose advice angered the Lord), God made him more prosperous than he was before (Job 42:10).

King Nebuchadnezzar told Shadrach, Meshach and Abednego that they would be thrown into a blazing hot furnace if they didn't worship his image or serve his gods. They had the choice to either disobey God or die. They couldn't avoid the problem and had a monumental test of their faith. Would we demonstrate the same amount of trust in God? They chose the furnace and what do you suppose they were feeling as they were being tied up and thrown in?

On the other hand, Peter failed his test. After weeping with despair from denying Christ three times (Luke 22:62), Peter had to be emotionally and spiritually heartbroken. However, he was given other opportunities to make known his association with Jesus. Peter boldly preached about Him, but not without physical persecution (Acts 5:40). To be "flogged" means to be beaten harshly with a whip or rod. It was used as a punishment to inflict pain and torture on people - much worse than imprisonment with chains, which Peter also endured.

God told Ananias that Paul would suffer for His name.[49] Indeed, Paul experienced many hardships and much pain. He was flogged, exposed to death, beaten, stoned, shipwrecked, whipped, and constantly in danger. He was sleep deprived, hungry and thirsty, cold, naked, and daily faced pressures and concerns.[50] Perhaps the thing that bothered Paul the most was what he called "the thorn in my flesh" that tormented him. "Three times I pleaded with the Lord to take it away from me" (2 Corinthians 12:7-8). He did more than mention the problem, he begged the Lord to take it away, but the Lord wanted him to live with it. So Paul looked for the good in that trouble and trusted that God's power would rest on him because of his weakness.

Jesus Christ experienced so much pain and sorrow that He asked His Father for relief. Jesus, without exaggerating, told his disciples that His soul was "overwhelmed with sorrow to the point of death." The Bible says that He was deeply distressed and troubled.[51] And that was just mentally knowing what was going to happen to Him. He still had to physically experience it. Jesus was unjustly flogged, stripped, mocked and spat at, and repeatedly struck before being crucified – an excruciating, shameful way to die. But there is more. He had to endure separation from God to fully take the punishment of man's sin.

What makes us think that we should be exempt from pain, sorrow, trouble, and tears when even Jesus, who never sinned, had to suffer? Why do we get mad at God when problems come our way? (Sometimes, it is our own fault!) God never wastes pain; He always uses it to accomplish His purpose. And His purpose is for our ultimate good. Read Hebrews 5:7-9. During the days of Jesus' life on earth, what did He do? (vs. 7)

> *God never wastes pain; He always uses it to accomplish His purpose.*

_____

_____

What did He learn from His suffering? (vs. 8) _____

What is our benefit? (vs. 9) _____

_____

Read Isaiah 38:17 in the inset. What did King Hezekiah say about the purpose of his pain?

_____

> **"Surely it was for my benefit that I suffered such anguish."**
> **Isaiah 38:17**

These biblical people suffered, but also trusted God and prayed for help. Hopefully, you have read and know the rest of each story that was referred to. We see good endings for everyone mentioned. There are many more examples in the Bible which demonstrate people having to trust God through their troubles and tears. And it is a common occurrence for every person on earth.

Prayer For Today:

Thank God that He is faithful to those who suffer, but still trust Him.

Ask God to help you trust Him and to anticipate the good that will come from your trial.

_____

_____

_____

Day Two: Today's Troubles

Do you know people who think they are worse off than everybody else and are comfortable pitying themselves? In Job 5:7, we read that "man is born to trouble as surely as sparks fly upward." Sometimes, when we compare our troubles to those in the Bible, our adversities don't seem so bad. What present heartache or problems are you experiencing right now?

_____

_____

Some of our troubles are sudden and traumatic like losing a job without warning, accidents, heart attacks, strokes, and unexpected deaths. Other problems are chronic, persistent, and seemingly wear us down over time. Examples of these can be migraines, cancer and other diseases, financial struggles, and strong-willed children. In addition to our own emotional pain, sometimes we're called to help bear the pain of others. This can include immediate or extended family, friends, neighbors, and fellow church members.

Major catastrophes are happening all over the world. Earthquakes, tsunamis, hurricanes, tornadoes, drought, floods, fires, and plagues are occurring with more frequency. Terrorism has exploded—torture, rape, and mass killings—demonstrating that cruelty and evil are rampant.

On a much smaller scale, those whose lives are free from major issues still experience frustrating events of daily life, which rob us of our peace of mind. There are many examples of this: misbehaving pets, illness, car trouble, broken washing machine or vacuum, spats with a significant other, loss of electricity for days, an over-demanding and never satisfied boss, unpaid bills, computer viruses, lost cell phone, and malfunctioning plumbing the day company arrives. I'm sure you could name some more...

God's creation was perfect until Adam and Eve's disobedience to God brought evil and death into the world. All of creation was affected and every person inherited an innate nature to sin. Some suffering may be the result of living in a fallen, broken world or perhaps the natural consequence of making sinful choices. Other suffering could be the supernatural work of Satan; Satan was responsible for Job's suffering. Yet, God rules over the good and the bad. He is never caught by surprise when trouble comes our way, but knows all things and has control over our circumstances. We see only a small part of the whole picture, just one aspect of God's big plan.

It's difficult to trust God when life hurts because we get discouraged so easily. The Bible addresses this issue often, advising us to turn to the Lord. It is interesting to see how many times the same exhortation is given between people, particularly leaders. The following verses are very similar in content—instructing others not to be afraid or discouraged, but to be strong and courageous because the Lord will be with them. In each of these verses, tell who is <u>giving</u> this advice, and who is <u>receiving</u> it.

Deuteronomy 31:7-8 _____

Joshua 1:1,9 _____

Joshua 10:24-25 _____

1 Chronicles 22:7,13 _____

2 Chronicles 20:15,17 _____

Between God and Israel and Israel's leaders, we see that this advice is repeated. Each recipient had a real cause for concern, and by experiencing God's faithfulness, they learned how to trust in their Lord and deliver the same message they had received.

> "In this world you will have trouble. But take heart! I have overcome the world."
> John 16:33

Why doesn't God spare us from trouble or heartache or disease? When things are going well for us, we tend to forget about God because we don't need Him as much. But when difficulties, injustice, and confusion appear, we want His help, and pray more fervently. When good comes out of our troubles, we can credit God and praise Him. When we see His wisdom and goodness through our problems, we worship and thank Him for answering our prayers. When we thank God and praise Him, and when we tell others how faithful and good God is, we glorify Him. And we are told to glorify God. If we don't need God and live independently from Him, we'll have nothing to testify about.

Read James 1:2. We are told to consider it joy whenever we face trials of many kinds. Notice the word "whenever" is used, not "if." There will be trials and problems in every Christian's life. God never said He would prevent our troubles, but He will help us through them. Read John 16:33 in the inset. What does this passage say about trouble?

_____

_____

What did Jesus say in Matthew 6:34?

_____

_____

God allowed several medical problems in my life. A pinched nerve in my neck shot pain down my shoulder, arm, and into my fingers on my right hand, which eventually became numb. I needed surgery to replace some vertebrae and disk damage in my neck. The operation did not eliminate all of the pain and I developed fibromyalgia. The fatigue and weakness associated with this disease is overwhelming, and the linked muscular and joint pain generates many tears.

I know why God let this happen. I was determined to do everything in my own strength and God wanted to teach me a lesson. He made me so pathetic that I had no other choice than to turn to Him and rely on Him totally. And when I finally understood and complied, God showed me what He could do for me. Whenever I served Him - like leading a Bible study group - He took away my pain and fatigue from the minute I started until I walked out of the room or church. His power was made known and seen through my weakness, week after week. I eventually learned how to handle fibromyalgia in my body and I have improved, but never to the point where I don't need God's assistance, be it mental or physical. Taking away my health and requiring God's help has taught me who is in control and who is not. But it also made me realize His love for me and what He did to get my full dependence on Him. That new reliance initiated an intimate relationship with the Lord and has blessed me more than I could ever imagine. If I never had all that pain to start with, I probably would have wasted many more years of my life without feeling God's love in my heart, His power in my body, and the joy of serving Him in a whole new way.

When we are in the midst of hardships or fear, trusting God has to be a conscious effort. We should be aware that although we don't know the future or all the facts that pertain to our problems, God does. And since He loves us and knows what is best for us at any given time, we need to trust Him.

Has there ever been an occasion when God did not give you what you asked for (because He is so wise), and later you were grateful that He didn't? Examples can be a certain job, house, or even a spouse. Perhaps you later realized how terrible it could have been if God granted your request. Or maybe you recognized how wonderful everything turned out even though you were despondent that God did not appear to be acting on your behalf.

Christians will probably suffer from injustice or persecution. God never promised that life would be easy or fair; in fact, He said just the opposite. Jesus talked about the trials and problems we would have, and used the same phrase in all of these verses: Matthew 10:38, 16:24, Mark 8:34, Luke 9:23. What is that phrase? _____

> *When life gets difficult, one needs to pray to the Father for help in getting through the situation, not expect to avoid it completely.*

Cross-bearing is a willingness to suffer and die for the Lord's sake. This arises from our loyalty to God and Jesus Christ. In Luke's account, Jesus mentioned that this is a daily action of obedience and self-denial. Jesus explained that if a person is not willing to suffer or carry his cross and follow Him, he/she cannot be His disciple.[52] Following the Lord takes commitment. When life gets difficult, one needs to pray to the Father for help in getting through the situation, not expect to avoid it completely. Furthermore, Jesus wants to help us through those rough times and instructed us to go to Him for comfort and encouragement.

In 2 Corinthians 1:3, how did Paul describe God our Father? _____

_____

How did Jeremiah describe God? Jeremiah 8:18 _____

Whom does God comfort? Isaiah 49:13 _____

Matthew 5:4 _____

2 Corinthians 7:6 _____

"For just as the sufferings of Christ flow over into our lives, so also through Christ our comfort overflows" (2 Corinthians 1:5). Fill in the blanks for Matthew 11:28-29.

"_____ to me, all you who are _____ and

_____, and I will give you _____. Take

my _____ upon you and _____ from me,

for I am _____ and _____ in heart, and you

will find _____ for your _____."

David understood this because he proclaimed, "Praise be to the Lord, to God our Savior, who daily bears our burdens" (Psalm 68:19).

Prayer For Today:

Thank God that He is able to comfort you through your struggles and problems.

Ask God for comfort and guidance as you endure your current trial or sorrow.

_____

_____

_____

Day Three: Reasons For Troubles

If God is loving, wise, and sovereign, why does He allow us to have so much adversity in our lives? If He is so good, why does He permit famine or evil to triumph? We must remember that God created a perfect world, but man's choice to disobey Him affected all of His creation. Yet, this damaged world we live in is temporary, and God is preparing us for our eternal life with Him. Those who have accepted Jesus as Lord and Savior look forward to heaven where there is no more pain and sorrow. In the meantime, let's find out some reasons behind our personal troubles and tears. Write the correct letter (representing the reason why we experience difficulties) in front of the verse that references it.

_____ John 15:2	a.	Holiness
_____ Acts 1:8	b.	Pruning
_____ Romans 5:3	c.	Dependence on God
_____ 2 Corinthians 1:9b	d.	Praise to God
_____ 2 Corinthians 6:18	e.	Witness
_____ 2 Corinthians 9:12	f.	Perseverance
_____ Hebrews 12:10	g.	Relationship to God
_____ James 1:12	h.	Testing of Faith
_____ 1 Peter 1:7	i.	Service

Holiness. God calls us to live a holy life (2 Timothy 1:9). 1Peter 1:14-16 helps explain why.

> As obedient children, do not conform to the evil desires you had when you lived in ignorance. But just as he who called you is holy, so be holy in all you do; for it is written; "Be holy, because I am holy."

God commanded His people to be holy amid other instructions from Mt. Sinai.[53] This was one way they would be identified as His people. God's command was extended to all believers in Christ when the Holy Spirit was given to men. Sanctification is a process of becoming holy, set apart from the world and for God. As we strive to be Christ-like and serve Him because we love Him and want to please Him, our minds are slowly transformed to desire the things of God, and thus the process of sanctification occurs. Even though we cannot escape sin in our lives, we can certainly desire holiness and be sanctified with the Holy Spirit's help.

No one likes to be disciplined, but for our own good and out of His love, God works to instill holiness in us.

The process of being made holy by the work of the Holy Spirit in the lives of Christians is sometimes called "progressive sanctification." Being declared holy through belief in Christ's atoning death on the cross is "positional sanctification."[54] God desires both for us. He uses the situations we face each day to weave a pattern of godliness into our character. He has been working quietly and patiently throughout our lives.

The author of Hebrews 12:10 explained that the Lord disciplines us for our good, so that we might share in His holiness. Discipline is corrective training that produces righteousness and peace (Hebrews 12:11). It typically exposes our sinful nature, leads us to confess and repent, and consequently grow in holiness. Discipline can be in many forms, but it usually causes us to hurt enough to change our ways. In Hebrews 12:6 and Proverbs 3:12, we read that the Lord disciplines those He loves. No one likes to be corrected, but through God's love, He works in us to instill holiness and to keep us from greater harm. Any path that believers travel which detours from our sanctification will be blocked with discipline. It usually comes after we ignore all the road signs alerting us to the change in route we've taken. The purpose is to stop our erroneous ways (which eventually lead us to fall into a pit) and adjust our course to journey in the right direction.

Fill in the blanks for 1 Thessalonians 4:7.

"For _____ did not call us to be _____, but to

live a _____ _____."

Pruning may take you by surprise; something you don't want to let go of is taken away.

Pruning. To further understand this analogy, we need to read John 15:1-5. God our Father is the gardener who cares for the branches of His vine in order to make them fruitful. The branches represent Christians, and the grapes symbolize their fruitfulness in serving God. When tending grapevines, fruitful branches are cut back or pruned to promote growth and more fruit. The analogy is that God will loosen our grip on things that impede our devotion and service to Him. He removes anything that stunts our spiritual maturity and growth. His purpose is to strengthen our character and faith so we may be fruitful and glorify Him. Pruning may take us by surprise; something we don't want to let go of is taken away. It hurts, and we may even feel impaired, but in the long run, pruning increases fruitfulness. This fruitfulness has its own rewards, for obeying and serving the Lord provides benefits such as answered prayer and joy (John 15:7,11).

Good fruit represents the product of a godly life – virtues of character (inner fruit) and good works. This fruit is distinguishable, because Jesus advised, "by their fruit you will recognize them" (Matthew 7:16). According to verse 17, He added, "Likewise every good tree bears good fruit, but a bad tree bears bad fruit." God desires good fruit from our lives, the fruit of serving God in action and developing our character - the fruit of the Spirit. Remember that the fruit of the Spirit is love, joy, peace, patience, kindness, goodness, faithfulness, gentleness and self-control. Which of the 9 inner fruit needs maturing in your life? _____

What additional fruit is mentioned in Philippians 1:11? _____

These virtues of character bring God glory, honor, and praise while it prepares us for eternal life with Him. Jesus declared, "This is to my Father's glory, that you bear much fruit" (John 15:8). Anything that gets in the way of this, God will prune out of the Christian's life.

Dependence on God. We acknowledge that God wants a personal relationship with us, but to what length will He go to motivate us into wanting one with Him? Allowing a person to suffer – physically, emotionally, or mentally – creates a desire for God's help, which in turn, initiates a renewed or closer relationship with Him. God wants us to need Him, to depend on Him and not ourselves. Paul explained that the hardships they suffered occurred so they would not rely on themselves, but on God who raises the dead, and is able to do anything (2 Corinthians 1:9b). God desires our trust and dependence on Him for our needs, direction, and future.

> *God desires our trust and dependence on Him for our needs, direction, and future.*

There are several ways to depend on God. Besides approaching the Lord with our questions and problems, we rely on Him for effectiveness in our service rather than on our own energy, effort, or talent. He wants us to proclaim, "I can do everything through Him who gives me strength" (Philippians 4:13). When we depend on the Lord, we put our hope in Him—hope that He will enable us in the present, and hope that He will be faithful to us in the future. Let's look at Isaiah 40:28-31. What does our Creator God give to the weary?

_____

What does He do for the weak? _____

What happens to those who hope in the Lord? _____

_____

God is never too busy or tired to help us. He wants us to come to Him, ask for help, and experience His lovingkindness. Let's say a hungry little boy is leaning over the table struggling to make a peanut butter and jelly sandwich. His parent observes him getting upset and wants to assist him, but waits for him to ask for help. It is so simple for the parent, yet the child becomes frustrated and quits trying without ever looking up from the table to request aid. Then he walks away still hungry. Likewise, our Father in heaven doesn't want us to quit when we become frustrated in life, but is waiting for us to look up and ask Him for help. He is ready and willing. We do not have because we do not ask God.[55]

Read what Jesus said in Matthew 7:11 and fill in the blanks.

"If you, then, though _____ are evil, know how to give good

_____ to your _____, how much more will

your _____ in heaven _____ good _____

to _____ _____ _____ him!"

God's gifts to His children include strength, guidance, provision, healing, protection, wisdom, peace, joy, and grace. Can you name some more? _____

Read Romans 12:12 and fill in the blanks, quoting Paul, who was not afraid to ask for help.

"Be_____in_____,_____

in_____,_____in_____."

When we are faithful in prayer and ask the Lord for His help and guidance, we can be patient in affliction and better able to endure the inevitable hardships in our lives. Our hope and trust gives us comfort that God is in control and is able to bring something good out of our troubles. After all, He loves us and wants the best for us. That's why we can depend on Him.

Prayer For Today:

Thank God that He is sovereign and orchestrates good out of our troubles and tears.

Ask God to help you realize what He desires of you when you experience adversity.

_____

_____

_____

Jesus told us in Matthew 7:16 that we will recognize people by their fruit. I told my adult children not to judge others but to be fruit inspectors as they look for their spouses. Look for the fruit of the Holy Spirit in the other person's life that gives witness to their relationship with Jesus Christ. Anyone can call himself a Christian, but true Christians show evidence of their faith. Hopefully, we all demonstrate this fruit in our own lives too.

We'll continue exploring God's tolerance of suffering in part two of Reasons for Troubles.

Day Four: Reasons For Troubles Part 2

Let's review. What were the three reasons already discussed why God allows adversity in our lives?

_____

_____

Praise to God. What does the word "praise" mean to you?

_____

_____

Praising God means to give honor to Him. How often do we praise Him? I mean really praise Him with exuberant joy? When we are suffering and in tears, praise is not the first thing on our minds. Yet, when we trust God to deliver us, and He is faithful and does "immeasurably more than all we ask or imagine" (Ephesians 3:20), gratitude and joy fill our hearts. We praise Him with hope in the midst of our troubles, and with thanksgiving afterwards. We rejoice in His love and power, and praise Him that our next life will be glorious. In 1Peter 1:6-7 we read:

> In this you greatly rejoice, though now for a little while you may have had to suffer grief in all kinds of trials. These have come so that your faith…may be proved genuine and may result in praise, glory and honor when Jesus Christ is revealed.

God allows us to experience adversity so that afterwards, when we notice His help and goodness to us, He can be praised. Unlike the nine lepers who never returned to thank Jesus for their healing, we need to be like the one who had gratitude in his heart and "came back, praising God in a loud voice. He threw himself at Jesus' feet and thanked him…" (Luke 17:15-16). Have you been blessed with a miracle of healing? Praise God! Has He answered a prayer for you that had been troubling you for some time? Praise His name! Did He turn that unfair situation into something great? Praise the Lord!

Mary and Martha could not understand why Jesus allowed their brother to die. Why didn't He hurry to get there and heal him? Though we suffer and do not understand God's plans, we certainly can praise and glorify Him for the end results. Jesus told the sisters, "Did I not tell you that if you believed, you would see the glory of God?"[56] He then brought Lazarus back to life after being dead for four days. That event justified praise and rejoicing, giving honor and glory to God!

Can you praise God when you do not observe any good? It is difficult to say to the Lord, "I praise You even though I am hurting and don't understand why You are allowing this." Paul instructed us to "Rejoice in the Lord always. I will say it again: Rejoice!" (Philippians 4:4). Peter, Paul, and James all mentioned rejoicing when suffering for being a Christian. The apostles considered it an honor to suffer for Jesus Christ. Habakkuk learned to trust in God

Acknowledgement of God's past help, with the promise of a glorious future eternal life, enables us to praise the Lord in all circumstances.

regardless of his circumstances. He declared that even if God should send suffering and loss, he would still rejoice in God his Savior. Read Habakkuk 3:17-18 below.

> Though the fig tree does not bud and there are no grapes on the vines, though the olive crop fails and the fields produce no food, though there are no sheep in the pen and no cattle in the stalls, yet I will rejoice in the Lord, I will be joyful in God my Savior.

David praised God throughout his psalms. He had his share of difficulties; yet, he was so thankful for God's blessings. Psalm 103:1-6 records David's grateful heart. From verse 1, what part of David praised the Lord? _____

What should we not forget? (vs. 2) _____

What are the benefits we experience?

(vs. 3) _____

(vs. 4) _____

(vs. 5) _____

(vs. 6) _____

David's life was full of turmoil, and even in the bad times, he trusted God and praised Him with his inmost being for the gifts God had already given to him. No matter how difficult our life's journey is, we can always be thankful for God's blessings that we take for granted. Recorded in 1 Thessalonians 5:18, what did Paul encourage us to do? Fill in the blanks below.

"give _____ in _____ circumstances, for this is _____ _____ for _____ in Christ Jesus."

Acknowledgement of God's past help in one's life, with the promise of a glorious future eternal life, enables one to praise the Lord in all circumstances.

Witness. Could you imagine living during Jesus' time on earth? Would you have been one in the crowd that followed Him, or a devout Pharisee or Sadducee that criticized Him from jealousy? Maybe you'd be like Zacchaeus, just wanting to see Him. In any case, you would have been an eyewitness. No photos or pictures of Jesus exist, just His words and those of His apostles. It's amazing how those words have changed the world. The Holy Spirit still uses them to change people today. Some of those words spoken by Jesus tell us to witness for Him. Tell the gospel story, yes, but also witness or testify to His goodness, faithfulness, and love. We are to share our faith, our testimonies of how the Lord has been active in our lives. "Come and listen, all you who fear God; let me tell you what he has done for me" (Psalm 66:16).

According to Acts 1:8, Jesus gave some parting words to His disciples before they watched Him rise into the sky. He told them that the Holy Spirit would come on them and they would be His witnesses locally in Jerusalem, further away into Judea and Samaria, and to the ends of the world. So the formerly uneducated fishermen went about preaching with the power of the Holy Spirit, and effectively witnessed.

Witnessing involves showing and telling what God has done for us. (And we thought "show and tell" was only for little ones.) Sometimes our problems bring attention to God's power. The disciples asked Jesus whose sin caused a man's blindness. Jesus answered that it wasn't sin; the blindness was "so that the work of God might be displayed in his life" (John 9:3). And He healed the blind man. From Luke 8:38-39, what did Jesus instruct a grateful, healed man to do?

_____

Furthermore, our faith in Jesus Christ enables us to experience the power of the Holy Spirit in our lives, which in itself, gives us something to witness about. And it's both exciting and encouraging to see and hear about God's power in people's lives.

Three different times Paul asked God to make him well by removing his affliction. In 2 Corinthians 12:9, God replied, "My grace is sufficient for you, for my power is made perfect in weakness." The Living Bible states God's answer as this: "No. But I am with you; that is all you need. My power shows up best in weak people." Although God did not remove Paul's physical problem, He said He would demonstrate His power in Paul. And Paul's response was that he would boast all the more gladly about his weaknesses, so that Christ's power may rest on him.

When we are confident in our own ability or have many resources, we tend to serve God and do things in our own strength. But if we are weak and allow God to fill us with His power, we become stronger than we could ever be on our own. It's like being on spiritual steroids. When God's power is displayed through our weaknesses and we become aware of Him working through us, life becomes exciting. We get energized and trust God more because the truth we believe is confirmed with experience. Like Paul, we can witness about our inadequacies and how God works in us and through us, and praise and honor Him in the process. As a consequence, others see God in us, just as the Jewish rulers and teachers saw God's power in Jesus' disciples.[57] They went through the villages, preaching the gospel and even performed miracles![58] When have you witnessed to others about God's power in your life?

_____

What was the reaction of your listeners? _____

> *Believers are called to be living witnesses and to testify about God's power in their lives.*

When God does the unexpected, unexplainable, or unbelievable in our lives, we need to share our joyful experience so that others may be encouraged and their hope be restored. The focus is on God's love and power, not ourselves. God changes hearts, heals incurable diseases, and provides for our needs when our resources are depleted. We should tell others how He worked behind the scenes to help us during our difficulties, or how He turned our troubles into triumphs. Our fellow believers and unbelievers need us to give evidence to and speak out when God demonstrates His faithfulness and grace.

Besides sharing verbally what God has done for us, we can witness by the way we live. Our lives can be a shining example to others when they watch us how we handle our problems. Read 1 Timothy 4:12 in the inset. What did Paul tell Timothy to do?

_____

_____

_____

> "Don't let anyone look down on you because you are young, but set an example for the believers in speech, in life, in love, in faith and in purity."
> 1 Timothy 4:12

We are to live in such a way that others see Christ in us. What kind of witness are you giving? Are you the light of the world? Are you letting your light shine before men (Matthew 5:14-16)? Would others desire a relationship with Jesus from observing your life?

Our troubles and tears cause us to be more appreciative of God's divine interventions and help, and that appreciation creates an excitement and desire to tell others about it. Believers are called to be living witnesses and to testify about God's power in their lives. This encourages others in their faith, especially when they are experiencing adversity.

Perseverance. Are you a quitter? Do you give up easily? Or are you more determined to stay the course, no matter what comes up against you? Hebrews 10:36 reveals why we need to persevere. Fill in the blanks to complete the verse.

"You _____ to _____ so that when you have

done the _____ of God, you will _____ what

he has _____ ."

God always keeps His promises because He is completely faithful. If God calls you to a particular service, He will equip you. Pursue that call and persevere in spite of obstacles and difficulties. Satan will try to throw as much opposition as He can to stop you, but God will supply what you need to complete the job and reward you for your obedience.

The author of Hebrews 12:1 encouraged believers to run with perseverance the race marked out for them. The Christian life is pictured as a long distance race or marathon. Life is hard and we will get tired. The path may be bumpy; Christians that are persecuted for their faith require an extra measure of perseverance to endure.

God allows injustice and persecution because one's perseverance and spiritual commitment are tested through the process. In Romans 5:3-5, we read that godly character traits are developed only through the tough times. Why did Paul say we should rejoice in our sufferings? (:3)

_____

A Christian can rejoice in suffering because he knows that it is not meaningless. What does perseverance produce? _____ What does character produce in us? _____ Does hope disappoint us? _____

Let's also look at James 1:2-4 below.

> Consider it pure joy, my brothers, whenever you face trials of many kinds, because you know that the testing of your faith develops perseverance. Perseverance must finish its work so that you may be mature and complete, not lacking anything.

James recognized that perseverance matures our faith. According to James 5:10-11, which people did James want remembered as an example of patience in the face of suffering?

_____

What person did James refer to for his perseverance? _____

Peter claimed that the virtues listed in 2 Peter 1:5-9 would produce a fruitful Christian life. What virtues did he include?

_____

_____

What happens if you possess those qualities in increasing measure?

_____

_____

"Blessed is the man who perseveres under trial, because when he has stood the test, he will receive the crown of life that God has promised to those who love him."
James 1:12

The great apostles Paul, James, and Peter persevered through their trials and testified that God enabled them to endure the hard times. We don't have to face our problems alone. The Lord strengthens us and gives us peace and comfort through our troubles. As we persevere, we are blessed by God and encouraged to complete our marathon on earth well.

Read James 1:12 in the inset. Why is the man who perseveres through his trials blessed?

_____

_____

Prayer For Today:

Thank God that He wants to help you in your weakness by giving you His power. Even when you can't see the good, you can praise God for your past blessings and for your future reward.

Ask God for help in persevering through your difficulties and to focus on His sovereignty and faithfulness.

_____

_____

_____

We have three more reasons in Part Three tomorrow.

Day Five: Reasons For Troubles Part 3

Again, let's review. What three reasons for our troubles were discussed in the last lesson?

1. _____ 2. _____ 3._____

What three reasons were discussed two lessons ago?

1. _____ 2. _____ 3._____

Today, we will discuss the last three.

Relationship to God. Do you get mad or angry with God when He allows you to have painful, sorrowful, or stressful experiences? Do you complain about the amount or frequency of them? Do you get upset and cry out to Him when you encounter the rough times? Read Psalm 34:17. What does the Lord do for the righteous who cry out?

_____

_____

> Our relationship with the Lord will deepen if we turn to Him in our troubles and tears.

In Psalm 34:18, David expressed what he knew personally, "The Lord is close to the brokenhearted and saves those who are crushed in spirit." Our relationship with the Lord will deepen if we turn to Him in our troubles and tears.

Do you know the Lord so intimately that you can trust Him in any situation? Do you have complete assurance of His love for you? Is your faith strong enough to handle any disappointment, sadness, injustice, or pain? If not, there is room for growth.

The Lord orchestrates our spiritual development; He draws us closer to Himself through the tough times so that we learn more about Him directly. He wants us to personally experience His comfort, love, peace, and power. In other words, He desires a relationship with us. God confirms this in 2 Corinthians 6:18 where it is written, "I will be a Father to you, and you will be my sons and daughters, says the Lord Almighty." God initiates this relationship. His love is so great for us that He calls us His children, and He chooses to be a faithful, loving Father to us. "You received the Spirit of sonship. And by him we cry, 'Abba, Father.'" Read Romans 8:15-17. From verse 16, what does the Holy Spirit testify with our spirit? _____

In verse 17, Paul claimed that if we are God's children, then we are heirs of God and co-heirs with Christ. If we share in his sufferings, what else will we share? _____

_____

God promises that He will be with us in our difficulties and sorrows. If He doesn't prevent a problem from occurring, He supplies help (sometimes through other people) and the Spirit to fill us with His presence - giving us His peace and strength to persevere. God tells us not to fear, for "I am with you; do not be dismayed, for I am your God. I will strengthen you and help you; I will uphold you with my righteous right hand" (Isaiah 41:10). What did David profess in Psalm 23:4? _____

_____

This psalm is a reference to the Lord being our shepherd; shepherds use rods and staffs to care for and protect their sheep. Jesus also identified Himself: "I am the good shepherd; I know my sheep and my sheep know me – just as the Father knows me and I know the Father – and I lay down my life for the sheep" (John 10:14-15).

Jesus connects with us so closely that when we hurt, He hurts. Remember when the Lord called out to Saul (later renamed Paul) on the road to Damascus? Read Acts 9:4-5. What did He ask Saul in verse 4?

_____

And what was the Lord's reply about His identity to Saul in verse 5?

_____

Jesus is such a part of His believers, that He claims Saul was persecuting Him. How can this be?

In the New Testament, Jesus was visible and tangible. Before He ascended into heaven, He promised that the Holy Spirit would live in all those who believed in Him to be Lord and Savior. The Holy Spirit is part of the Trinity; He is one with God the Father and Jesus Christ the Son. When the Holy Spirit resides in believers, He bonds with them, and they become united. Even though the Spirit is not visible, believers are aware of His presence by His activity in their lives. And He is very aware of what is happening with those He indwells.

When life is good, we don't need God as much and we tend to spend less time communicating with Him. He occasionally uses pain and stress to bring us back to Him. Our

Father in heaven wants our love and attention, and for us to stay close to Him. He desires an intimate relationship with us.

Testing of Faith. Are you good at taking tests? Tests in any form - written, oral, or character - reveal what you don't know and expose your weaknesses. When my faith or character is tested and I'm deficient in some area, I become aware of it and learn where I need improvement.

Read James 1:12-13. We understand from verse 12 that people are tested and rewarded later. But in verse 13, there is an important clarification. Being tested and tempted are two different things. Our own evil desires may entice us or Satan tempts us in order to make us fail, but God never tempts anyone because He is holy. Instead, God may test us in order to confirm our faith. From the following verses, identify who or what is tested.

Genesis 22:1 _____

Jeremiah 11:20 _____

Daniel 3:13-18 _____

> *Without testing, we would never know what we are capable of doing and where we need improvement.*

Our faith is tested for purity as fire tests gold and purifies the metal. It takes the heat of trials for the Christian to be purified. Through the refining process, our impurities surface and God removes anything that gets in the way of complete trust in Him. Peter explained, "These [trials] have come so that your faith - of greater worth than gold, which perishes even though refined by fire - may be proved genuine" (1 Peter 1:7). Without the testing of our faith, we will not be cleansed or purified, which enables us to become more like Christ.

Without testing, we would never know what we are capable of doing and where we need improvement. We can be comforted and confident as our faith is tested when we remember the treasure we have within us. There is help available from the Holy Spirit. Although Satan wants us to fail our tests, God is rooting for us and waiting to reward us.

My favorite analogy for our faith being tested is that one's faith is like the body's spiritual muscle. Similar to other muscles in our body, when it is exercised regularly, it develops and grows stronger. When it is never used, it becomes weak. So another reason for testing is that God desires our faith to be active and strong, and will bring occasions to exercise it.

Service. Whom are we to serve? (Deuteronomy 13:4) _____

How are we to serve? (2 Chronicles 19:9; Galatians 5:13) _____

_____

Why are we to serve? (Ephesians 4:12-13) _____

_____

Do you enjoy serving the Lord? _____ How are you presently serving Him?

_____

_____

What is your motive for doing this? _____

_____

Paul urged believers to serve the Lord our God faithfully, wholeheartedly, in fear of the Lord, and in love. As we serve the Lord in this way, we build up the body of Christ and become mature in our faith and character.

God has called you for a particular service; do you know what it is?

We should remember that the only ability God is looking for is one's availability. He will give us whatever we need to accomplish the task He chooses for us. God may already be using us without our realizing it. So many times just what we say can be such a blessing to others. Read 1 Peter 4:10 in the inset. How are we to use our gifts from the Lord?

_____

_____

> **"Each one should use whatever gift he has received to serve others, faithfully administering God's grace in its various forms."**
> **1 Peter 4:10**

In verse 11 Peter continued, "If anyone serves, he should do it with the strength God provides, so that in all things God may be praised." We will likely be asked to do something we think we aren't qualified for or able to accomplish, so that we have to go to God and request help and rely on Him to get the job done.

Sometimes, it takes a trial or difficulty in one's life before the service opportunity presents itself. We may be allowed to suffer emotionally or physically. We may lose our physical capabilities or health or someone we love. We may experience depression and gain insight in the recovery. God occasionally asks us to serve Him in a unique way and our troubles may qualify us for the job.

It is not uncommon for our heavenly Father to use us to comfort others who go through the same trial we are dealing with or have previously experienced. We have the knowledge of what the problem involves and the empathy to help another person through it. Having experienced the same difficulty increases our understanding and makes us suitable to be an encourager.

> *When God carries us through our problems, our appreciation and thankfulness to Him can be expressed by encouraging others in a similar situation.*

Paul's many adversities qualified him to share from experience that our God is a Father of compassion "who comforts us in all our troubles, so that we can comfort those in any trouble with the comfort we ourselves have received from God" (2 Corinthians 1:4). I wonder if the hard times of our lives would have been any easier if we knew that God allowed us to suffer them because later we would use those experiences for good.

"This service that you perform is not only supplying the needs of God's people but is also overflowing in many expressions of thanks to God."
2 Corinthians 9:12

When God carries us through our problems, our appreciation and thankfulness to Him can be expressed by encouraging others in a similar situation to keep their faith and hope. Often, when we receive help from other people in a time of need, we are so grateful that we want to pay it forward by helping someone else in their need. And God calls us to do so when we've been on the receiving end of His mercy.

Read 2 Corinthians 9:12 in the inset. When we help others, what two duties are accomplished by the service we perform?

_____

_____

_____

God will equip us to serve Him through helping others. And that might mean experiencing some trouble and tears of our own to prepare us for the task.

Prayer For Today:

Thank God for wanting a relationship with you and adopting you as His child.

Ask God to reveal a past trial from your life that you can use to encourage other people in their faith.

_____

_____

_____

CHAPTER FIVE DISCUSSION/REVIEW QUESTIONS

1. What trial or difficulty is presently in your life that's testing your faith and trust in God?

2. Why doesn't God spare us from heartache or disease?

3. How do you react when God doesn't give you what you ask for? How should we act?

4. What does it mean to "take up your cross and follow me"?

5. When was the last time you felt God's comfort?

6. What does it mean to be holy? How do we become holy?

7. What is the Father's goal for pruning in one's life? Why does it hurt to be pruned?

8. What are you depending on God for - at this stage of your life?

9. What has God done specifically for you that calls for praise?

10. Why is it difficult to praise God when you do not observe any good?

11. How often do you share with others what the Lord has done for you? (Psalm 66:16) What keeps you from testifying about His power and love?

12. What helps you persevere through your troubles?

13. What do you appreciate most in your relationship with the Lord?

14. What are the differences between being tempted and tested? Is one harder to deal with than the other?

15. Are you content with your service to the Lord? What past event in your life could you use to encourage or comfort another believer?

Chapter Six: Choosing To Trust God

Day One: Will Over Feelings

> "For men are not cast off by the Lord forever. Though he brings grief, he will show compassion, so great is his unfailing love. For he does not willingly bring affliction or grief to the children of men."
> Lamentations 3:31-33

Are you afraid to trust God? Do you think that all of your past mistakes and sins will cause God to punish you instead of help you? Or do you presume that God won't be interested in your little issues because He is busy with more important matters like warring nations? The truth is that God loves us and wants the best for us. Psalm 145:13 records that God is faithful and loving toward all He has made. He wants to be involved in our daily lives. Even in the midst of problems, God is working on our behalf, though there may be times when it doesn't seem like it. Our Father in heaven calls Himself, "the compassionate and gracious God…abounding in love" (Exodus 34:6).

Read Lamentations 3:31-33 in the inset. Does the Lord want to bring us grief or affliction? _____ Yet, He allows it for specific reasons. Remember that when we hurt, He hurts.

When we have adversity that produces tears, we need to take heart. "For our light and momentary troubles are achieving for us an eternal glory that far outweighs them all," (2 Corinthians 4:16-17). Our troubles may surely seem more than light and momentary to us. But God compares them to what we have waiting for us in eternity and He says they are light and short-lived in comparison!

There are times when our feelings are affected by the pain we endure or the deep emotions we experience. It's important to be aware that our feelings can be wrong and discernment is needed in our lives. Therefore, trusting God should not be a matter of our feelings, but of our will. Trusting God is a choice. When our emotions are running wild, or a situation causes us to instinctively react with fear, we have to consciously remind ourselves of biblical truths, like God's supremacy. Remembering or rereading God's words encourages us during our difficult times. Prayer engages the Holy Spirit to help us recall what we have studied and to remember what God has done for us in the past. Prayer brings God's peace, and is necessary to overcome negative feelings like self-pity, jealousy, anger, and greed. This process of deliberately trusting God reaps benefits.

As you experience problems and trust God through them, you will develop a history where you can look back and marvel as you see how God was present and faithful to you. When you encounter new trials, remember and replay in your mind those times that God helped you, and trusting God will become easier to do.

A good example of this is found in Numbers 13-14 where 12 spies were sent into Canaan. Ten of them came back reporting the impossibility of Israel defeating the powerful giants living there. They were so awed by the Canaanites' size that they let their feelings of hopelessness dictate their next actions. They exaggerated the facts and recommended not going into their promised land. However, the other two spies also acknowledged the large size of the people occupying that land, but did not impulsively react to their feelings. They chose to remember their history with God and focus on His past miracles and power displayed on their behalf. They willfully pushed aside their fear and trusted God to help them. They remembered that Israel had the Lord who does the impossible and would give them the victory. Those two spies, Joshua and Caleb, were rewarded for their decision to trust God and were the only ones who were allowed to witness Israel's victory over the Canaanites and live in that prosperous, promised land. On the other hand, the other ten spies focused on the crisis instead of the One who could help them. They ignored God's miracles they previously witnessed and gave in to their fear.

Don't we often do the same? We magnify the difficult situation over God's sovereignty, the problem instead of His power, and the trouble without trusting God. Whenever we become anxious from encountering adversity, we need to focus on our powerful and compassionate God.

What is written in Psalm 77:14 about God's power? _____

_____

It's important to remember when God has answered our prayers, healed or protected us, and turned a negative situation into something good. This attitude—choosing to trust rather than follow our unreliable feelings—allows us to act on our faith, which God rewards.

Even the great prophets allowed their feelings to dictate their actions. Look at Elijah in 1 Kings 18-19. At first he is confident, then he is a coward. Elijah knows he's on the nationwide hit list and meets Israel's King Ahab and challenges him along with 450 prophets of Baal to see whose God is real. Each side is to prepare an altar for sacrifice and call on their God to set fire to it. Elijah openly ridicules the prophets who receive no response from their god. He then invokes a spectacular display of God's power, and orders the convinced Israelites to seize and kill all of Queen Jezebel's false prophets. Ahab goes home and tells Jezebel what happened and she sends a threat to Elijah claiming the same fate for him within 24 hours. (He already was on the wanted list for being one of the Lord's prophets.) Yet, "Elijah was afraid and ran for his life" (1 Kings 19:3).

One angry woman scares this great prophet and has him running away and wishing he was dead! What happened to his courage? Where was the memory of the triumphant miracle God just performed? Elijah let his feelings of fear dictate his actions. He forgot God's power and fled, disregarding how God had provided for him in the past. Yet, God sent an angel to help him.

> *Fear is an emotion that surfaces when we forget God is on the throne and in control.*

How quickly do we panic and act apart from God? Fear is an emotion that surfaces when we forget God is on the throne and in control. Our attitudes toward our problems become less frightening when we remember our Creator's power, love, and faithfulness to us.

Name the people who erroneously let their emotions and feelings guide their actions.

Matthew 26:56 _____ (fear)

Judges 16:16-17 _____ (weariness)

Exodus 32:1 _____ (impatience)

Genesis 25:29-34 _____ & _____ (coveting and self-gratification)

Genesis 4:5-8 _____ (jealousy/anger)

Whenever you are being tested and face problems, you must exercise your faith and act on your beliefs, not your emotions. When you find yourself in trouble, seek the Lord's help. Jesus declared, "apart from me, you can do nothing" (John 15:5), and "all things are possible with God" (Mark 10:27). He wants you to come to Him.

From Psalm 34:4, what does the Lord do when we seek Him?

_____

_____

And from Psalm 34:15, how aware is the Lord of His people?

_____

_____

According to Psalm 34:17-18, how active is the Lord toward those who need Him?

_____

_____

Trusting God is a decision. It involves your will that is based on your knowledge of God and what you believe about Him. Regardless of how you feel, decide to act on your belief that God is wise, loving, and powerful. If you rely on His promises and remember what He has done for His people (including yourself) in the past, your hope will be renewed and trusting in the Lord will come more naturally.

Prayer For Today:

Thank the Lord that He is watching out for you and will answer you when you call.

Ask the Spirit to help you focus on God's power and past provisions when faced with a trial.

_____

_____

_____

Day Two: Excuses

If you haven't fully submitted yourself to the Lord and trusted Him yet, you might be wondering how to start. Since the ability to trust begins with knowledge of God and what one believes about Him, start by reading in the Bible about His faithfulness. Whether it's your first time or you refresh your memory, read about the events where God kept His word and how He displayed His wisdom, power, and love. Deliberately saturate your mind with the truths written by His eyewitnesses and the apostles - truths of our Lord God's trustworthiness and reliability. Ask the Holy Spirit to give you the Scripture that will erase your doubts and encourage you. Memorize those verses and speak them out loud. Repetition is an effective method of persuading the mind to accept a truth.

Jesus recited Scripture often; we should follow His example. The Word of God is powerful and active. We can counter any excuse for not trusting God with Bible verses. These are excuses I have heard – do you use them?

- I'm afraid to trust God. I read that He is a just God and will punish disobedience. Maybe God will discipline me instead of help me.

- God won't be interested in my concerns; He's got bigger and more important things to do than help me.

- I don't think God hears my prayers. He never gives me what I want.

- I screwed up before and just can't take the risk again.

- God is allowing people in the world to starve. He must not care or cannot do anything.

What excuses have you given to the Lord for not trusting Him and serving Him?

_____

I have found myself being lazy and not wanting to put forth the effort. I think other people are better qualified for a particular task. I have a fear of unknown results or of being a failure. And sometimes, I just don't like doing the type of work involved.

It's interesting to look at people in the Bible who made excuses not to serve God after He gave them an assignment. Basically, they didn't trust God enough to willingly comply. From these verses, who are these people?

Exodus 4:10-15 _____ and Judges 4:6-9 _____

Focusing on his weakness, Moses gave God an excuse not to serve. In response, God reminded Moses that He made his mouth and would help him speak and teach him what to say. Yet, Moses either didn't want to do that job or he didn't trust in God's power because he still asked Him to send someone else (which made the Lord angry).

The prophetess Deborah told Barak that God commanded him to go to battle and that God would give him the victory. That wasn't enough for Barak. He wanted Deborah to go with him. Barak's request showed that he trusted other humans more than God's word.

Jesus gave a parable of the great feast in Luke 14:16-24. What were the 3 excuses given?

☐ poor health   ☐ field work   ☐ expenses

☐ care for children   ☐ new livestock   ☐ care for parents

☐ too far to travel   ☐ marriage obligation

We see that the timing was inconvenient to the people that were called. Our excuses can sound reasonable—family obligations, finances, health, prior commitments—but God's call to come to Him and serve Him is more important than anything else. It may seem inconveniently timed, but He has everything under His perfect control. There are no justifiable excuses to give if one trusts the Lord; He will provide everything we need to accomplish the task requested of us.

Have you been making excuses to avoid responding to God's call? He doesn't need you, He just chooses you. If you keep making excuses, He will give the privilege to someone else and you will miss the blessing from serving God through His power.

There is an incident recorded in the Old Testament which relates what can happen when one trusts the Lord with his whole heart. Read 1 Samuel 17:23, 32-33, 45-49. Who was fearless because he had confidence in the Lord even when the circumstances appeared hopeless? _____ Notice that he didn't claim any glory for himself, but it was all in the power of the Lord God. And look at his reply to Saul in verses 34-37. What animals did he kill with his bare hands? _____ Once again, he gave all the credit to God (:37). David relied on his past experiences, remembering when he saw God's power working through him, and was able to trust God for the victory over an intimidating new enemy.

"But be sure to fear the Lord and serve him faithfully with all your heart; consider what great things he has done for you."
1 Samuel 12:24

We learn to trust the Lord one circumstance at a time. As we start to build an account with God, we see how faithful He is. Remembering how He has helped us in the past reinforces the fact that He is willing and able to help us now. If you have nothing personal to draw on, believe the Bible which accurately records how God helped His people. He is still the same sovereign God now as He was then. Read 1Samuel 12:24 in the inset. What did Samuel tell the Israelites to do and consider?

_____

_____

David relied on his past experiences with God to trust Him for the victory over Goliath. Joshua and Caleb relied on God's past help in battles and His promises that Canaan would be Israel's. We can take their experiences along with our own to build our trust in the Lord. If we learn to trust Him for the minor problems, we will be better prepared to trust Him through the major ones. We're not to allow fear as an excuse for not trusting God.

God loves to work through those who are willing to surrender themselves to Him and serve Him. All who have learned this submission enjoy witnessing His power and the results. Examples of this lifestyle (recorded in the New Testament) are Jesus' apostles. Their trust grew as they spent time with Jesus, learned from Him, and acted on what He taught them. They submitted their lives to Him and trusted Him as they served Him. What power did God give them as a result of their faith and submissive hearts (Acts 2:43; 19:11-12)?

_____

Even though God may choose not to execute physical miracles through you, you will receive blessings from trusting and serving Him. Those blessings will far exceed any effort you put into your service. When one submits cheerfully, God rewards the person and His rewards are wonderful. "For your work will be rewarded, declares the Lord" (Jeremiah 31:16). The apostle Paul advised, "Always give yourselves fully to the work of the Lord, because you know that your labor in the Lord is not in vain" (1Corinthians 15:58). With the right attitude and motivation in serving, you will always receive more than you give.

If Jesus repeatedly tells us to trust Him, why do we doubt Him or insist on having control and trying to do things our own way? Why do we try to justify our lack of faith with excuses? If we believe the Bible is true, there is no valid excuse for doubting God. And if we trust God, there is no acceptable excuse for not serving Him.

> It's much easier to handle emergencies when you already have a close relationship with the Lord and know His reliable promises.

No one has complete control over his/her life or knows what tomorrow may bring. Trying to manage one's own life without God leads to struggle and confusion. But when you put Jesus in the driver's seat of your life and take your hands off the steering wheel, He'll take you places you could never reach by yourself! "Submit yourselves, then, to God" (James 4:7).

Our sinful human nature wants to exercise control and do things our own way, so it takes a concerted effort to submit to God, to trust and obey Him. When we stay in daily contact with the Lord, we are less prone to create painful circumstances for ourselves. When we communicate with God daily, in other words, have an intimate relationship with our Lord, we are more likely to stay within His will. Through prayer and reading God's Word, we stay connected. It's much easier to handle emergencies when we already have a close relationship with the Lord and know His reliable promises. The underlying factor of that intimate relationship is a heart surrendered to the Lord.

Previously in this Bible study, you were encouraged to make a list of all the times you have seen God act on your behalf. Did you? Making that list and referring to it prevents excuses from being made. Are you adding to that list? I love my list for it is my written memory that can be reviewed whenever I start to doubt God. I remind myself of all the times God has displayed His power to me through healing, protection, answered prayers, and provision; He's even given me special insight to certain incidents. How quickly I forget when times get rough, and how wonderful it is to have something tangible to give me quick reassurance. Our God is always faithful!

When people step out and trust God, they will experience His faithfulness and won't make an excuse anymore. Taking that step may feel risky, but it will be worth it. God encourages us to trust Him and rewards us for doing so. We have nothing to lose by trying it, and everything to gain.

Prayer For Today:

Thank God that many historical events (recorded in the Bible) prove He's trustworthy.

Ask God to help you submit to His instructions and trust Him wholeheartedly.

_____

_____

_____

Day Three: When God Is Silent

I get frustrated with dropped phone calls. Sometimes I can be talking for a minute before I realize there is silence on the other end. Then I wonder how long ago the connection was lost and how much the other person had heard. "Can you hear me now?" used to be a popular saying for cell phone users. Have you ever felt like asking God that question? Why is it that some people seem to have a direct line to God and others can't get through or have lost their connection? Besides an answer of "wait" or "no," is God sometimes silent? Perhaps we should evaluate what else is going on when we think our prayers are being ignored. Let's consider some reasons for unanswered prayers.

• Unconfessed sin. Isaiah 59:1-2 states, "Surely the arm of the Lord is not too short to save, nor his ear too dull to hear. But your iniquities have separated you from your God; your sins have hidden his face from you, so that he will not hear." Whatever sinful action, impure thought, or unloving attitude has captivated you, confess it to the Lord, and repent. He already knows about it and is waiting to forgive you.

Did you know that the Lord probes your heart and mind, and examines you at night?[59] According to Psalm 139:23-24, what did David pray for the Lord to do?

_____

_____

Nothing is hidden from the Lord! If you can't remember your offenses, ask Him to reveal any unconfessed sin, and then help you correct any wrong attitude, thought, or behavior in your life. That prayer would be in God's perfect will, a prayer God likes to hear and answer.

When we evaluate our lives, we frequently experience amnesia concerning our sins. "If we claim to be without sin, we deceive ourselves and the truth is not in us. If we confess our sins, he is faithful and just and will forgive us our sins and purify us from all unrighteousness" (1John 1:8-9). God Himself reinforces this in 2 Chronicles 7:14-15. Read that passage in the inset. What do the people have to do for God to hear their prayer and forgive their sin?

_____

_____

> "If my people, who are called by my name, will humble themselves and pray and seek my face and turn from their wicked ways, then will I hear from heaven and will forgive their sin and will heal their land. Now my eyes will be open and my ears attentive to the prayers offered in this place."
> 2 Chronicles 7:14-15

• Unforgiving spirit. "And when you stand praying, if you hold anything against anyone, forgive him, so that your Father in heaven may forgive you your sins" (Mark 11:25). Someone may have lied about you or mistreated you. They may not be sorry nor ask for forgiveness, but you must forgive them anyway. Forgiving enables one to stop being angry or bitter and to move on. Forgiveness releases masked pain and allows healing. What does Hebrews 12:15 warn against? _____

_____

The Living Bible words it this way: "Watch out that no bitterness takes root among you, for as it springs up among you, it causes deep trouble, hurting many people in their spiritual lives." What does Romans 12:17, 19 advise you not to do?

_____

_____

What does Matthew 6:14-15 reveal about forgiveness?

_____

_____

Read the parable of the unmerciful servant in Matthew 18:21-35. What is Jesus' warning to His listeners after telling the story?

_____

_____

• Unbelieving heart. "Therefore I tell you, whatever you ask for in prayer, believe that you have received it, and it will be yours" (Mark 11:24). There is a link between faith and answered prayer. According to James1:6-7, James (half-brother of Jesus) asserted,

"But when he asks, he must _____ and _____

_____, because he who doubts is like a wave of the sea,

blown and tossed by the wind. That man should _____ think he
will _____ anything from the Lord."

We may fool many people but we cannot fool God. Our doubt may be great and our effort to pray may be half-hearted. Perhaps we should humble ourselves and get on our knees behind closed doors when we pray. We ought to ask God for more faith, like the man who asked Jesus for a miracle by healing his boy, that is, if Jesus could. Jesus' reply was, "If you can? Everything is possible for him who believes." So the father added to his request, "I do believe; help me overcome my unbelief!" (Mark 9:22-24). Many times we do not have because we do not ask.[60] Don't hesitate to ask the Lord to help you believe and trust in Him.

• Unacceptable motives. James also wrote, "When you ask, you do not receive, because you ask with wrong motives, that you may spend what you get on your pleasures" (James 4:3). We may have to search our hearts and ask ourselves why we desire something. Do we want to be served or to serve others? We sometimes make unwise requests. It is understandable that we cannot pray for anything immoral, unholy, or unacceptable to God. And even if we know what we want is morally okay, we still have to be submissive to Him in our prayers. Realizing that we don't know the reasons for many of our difficulties, and that God knows what is best for us, we pray for what we think we need, yet surrender to Him and His plan. So we pray for His will to be done, trusting it will result in something good. "This is the confidence we have in approaching God: that if we ask anything according to his will, he hears us. And if we know that he hears us – whatever we ask – we know that we have what we asked of him" (1John 5:14-15). Read Mark 14:35-36. What did Jesus pray in the garden of Gethsemane? _____

_____

_____

• Unresolved issues. The book of Malachi gives us three more reasons for unanswered prayers that involve our behavior which the Lord finds offensive. The first is when we are not trusting God in the financial area of our lives and we withhold our tithes and offerings, (Malachi 1:9; 3:8-10). The Lord expects our best in effort and to contribute to other people's needs generously. God was pleased with Abel's offering but not Cain's. Those brothers' spiritual attitudes were manifested in their offerings. What we give to the church or to other causes often reveals our disposition toward God. When we realize that everything we have is from Him, we respond by being good stewards of the money and possessions He entrusts to us. He desires a portion back in gratitude; thus, in obedience, we show honor and thanksgiving to Him by being generous. Our checkbooks and donated time can reflect how much we trust the Lord for our blessings and how grateful we are to Him for them. The right motive in giving is necessary for the Lord's approval and blessing.

Another behavioral reason for unanswered prayers is when we do not take care of the poor and oppressed among us (Malachi 3:5). There are many passages in the Bible that instruct us to help those in need and teach us that God blesses our obedience. So let's look at two examples of blessed, generous individuals who helped others. In Acts 9:36-41, the story of Tabitha is recorded. Tabitha was always doing good and helping the poor. What blessing did she receive?

In Acts 10:2-4, we read about Cornelius, a God-fearing Gentile who "gave generously to those in need and prayed to God regularly." An angel appeared to him and gave him a message. What came up as a memorial offering before God? _____

Read Acts 10:44-48 and notice that the blessing from his generosity was related to his faith. Cornelius and his family were among the first Gentiles to receive the Holy Spirit and be baptized.

Furthermore, God not only turns a deaf ear toward those who see a need and never respond, He also punishes them. Look what Matthew 25:41-45 reveals:

> Then he will say to those on his left, 'Depart from me, you who are cursed, into the eternal fire prepared for the devil and his angels. For I was hungry and you gave me nothing to eat, I was thirsty and you gave me nothing to drink, I was a stranger and you did not invite me in, I needed clothes and you did not clothe me, I was sick and in prison and you did not look after me.' They also will answer, 'Lord, when did we see you hungry or thirsty or a stranger or needing clothes or sick or in prison, and did not help you?' He will reply, 'I tell you the truth, whatever you did not do for one of the least of these, you did not do for me.'

The third case of improper behavior resulting in unanswered prayer is not being faithful to one's spouse (Malachi 2:14). Marriage is also discussed in the New Testament where Peter advised, "Husbands, in the same way be considerate as you live with your wives, and treat them with respect as the weaker partner and as heirs with you of the gracious gift of life, so that nothing will hinder your prayers" (1 Peter 3:7). According to Ephesians 5:33, what are husbands and wives each to do? _____

_____

- Undisclosed plans. The last consideration for unanswered prayer is that sometimes God's silence is part of His plan. Did you know that Jesus gave the silent treatment to certain people and refused to answer or speak? When He was in front of Herod, He remained quiet and didn't answer the questions put to Him (Luke 23:9). Jesus did not respond to the accusations from the crowd when He was on trial before the chief priests and elders, Pilate, and Caiaphas the high priest.[61] When Jesus knew His words wouldn't make a difference in a person's heart or when they could create a conflict with God's will for His life, He didn't waste His breath. Likewise, when God knows that you already have a hardened heart and won't change, or what you ask for opposes His plan for your life and holiness, He will be silent.

A sincere prayer with a submissive heart gets a response from God.

A sincere prayer with a submissive heart gets a response from God. "The Lord is far from the wicked but he hears the prayer of the righteous" (Proverbs 15:29). When the Lord hears our prayers, life can get exciting. There is power in prayer and prayer certainly makes a difference. Understand that the power of prayer is in the One who hears it, not the one who says it. Therefore, our prayer life is linked to our faith and trust in God.

Tomorrow, we will look at how to pray, some biblical heroes who combined their trust in God with prayer, and risking one's life.

Prayer For Today:

Thank God that He desires your prayers and conversation with Him.

Ask God to show you anything in your life that is hindering your prayers.

_____

_____

_____

Day Four: Why Pray?

Have you ever listened to a young child pray from his/her heart? It's so endearing. God feels the same way when His children (of all ages) speak to Him from their hearts.

James proclaimed that "the prayer of a righteous man is powerful and effective" (James 4:16). Are your prayers powerful and effective? What do you say to the Lord? Do your prayers sound the same day after day? Is your prayer mostly, "Dear God, please…" and then list the things you desire or think you need?

When you request something from God, what is your tone?

- ☐ like a person making a wish to a genie
- ☐ like a spoiled child demanding his way
- ☐ like a boss giving out orders to his employees
- ☐ like a student reciting a memorized sentence
- ☐ like a beggar asking a rich man for bread
- ☐ like a respectful child asking a loving father for help

> *The more time we spend communicating with God, the more intimate our relationship becomes, and our realization that we can trust Him grows.*

There are a variety of reasons why God wants us to pray. Prayer changes people. It dissolves negative attitudes like anger, bitterness, hatred, pride, selfishness, and a critical spirit. Prayer transforms our thoughts and conduct so we can love others. The more we pray, the more our thinking and behavior reflects Jesus. Prayer also removes our obstacles to being a servant of God. Paul told us to "devote ourselves to prayer" (Colossians 4:2). The more time we spend communicating with God, the more intimate our relationship becomes, and our realization that we can trust Him grows. From James 5:15, what two things does a prayer offered in faith do?

_____

Prayer is vital to Christianity. Our prayers should include:

- praise and worship
- confession of our sins and requesting forgiveness
- thanking God for answered prayers and other blessings
- intercession for others
- our own requests

Besides the model prayer which Jesus gave to us (Matthew 6:9-13), the Bible contains many more instructions on how to pray. What do these verses say about prayer?

Matthew 5:44 _____

It is easy to pray for people we love, but much more difficult to pray for our enemies. Jesus instructed His followers to "pray for those who mistreat you" (Luke 6:28). One way to repay evil with good is to pray for those who cause us grief.

Matthew 6:6 _____

Jesus said that anyone who prays to look good in front of others, but has no real relationship with God is a hypocrite, a pretender. Humble believers desire to talk with God personally and privately. Jesus "went up on a mountainside by himself to pray" (Matthew 14:23); He often withdrew to secluded places where He could talk to His Father.[62] Where do you pray most effectively? _____

Colossians 4:3 _____

Moses interceded for Israel and saved their lives. Jesus prayed for Peter's faith to remain strong and the apostles prayed for Peter while he was imprisoned. Paul prayed for the Philippians and asked for prayers from the Roman, Ephesian, Colossian, and Thessalonian believers with specific requests. James told us to "pray for each other so that you may be healed" (James 5:16). We are called to pray for other believers, our brothers and sisters in Christ.

1 Thessalonians 5:17 _____

Continually means without ceasing. In Ephesians 6:18, Paul encouraged us to pray in the Spirit on all occasions with all kinds of prayers and requests. We are to be alert and always keep on praying for all the saints. Day or night, anytime we happen to think of a need that should be addressed or a reason to praise God, we should talk to Him. Paul urged us to be "faithful in prayer" (Romans 12:12). According to Luke 18:1, what did Jesus tell His disciples and why? _____

_____

James 1:6a _____

We should pray expectantly. How much faith is in your prayers? _____

For those who have been taught to pray as a child, it can become more of a ritual at times, the required duty of a Christian. Yet, when we personally experience the power of God, our prayer life receives a boost and becomes more meaningful. Sometimes being a recipient of other people's prayers and God's mercy causes us to pray with more emotion and feeling.

There are times when we take our freedom to pray for granted. There are governments with laws that prohibit the freedom to worship God, and public prayer (especially in Jesus' name) is forbidden and can result in punishment. Daniel experienced this type of persecution when he was told that he could no longer pray to his God or he'd be thrown into the lion's den. This historical event is recorded in Daniel 6. In verse 10 we read, "three times a day he got down on his knees and prayed, giving thanks to his God, just as he had done before." Yet, God protected His faithful servant and rewarded him for his loyalty and trust.[63] That was quite a risk Daniel took - which others expected to result in death. But if we trust God whole-heartedly, we can take risks when it involves our faith and what God asks of us. We know that this life is temporary, but heaven is really our home. Jesus advised His followers:

> Do not let your hearts be troubled. Trust in God; trust also in me. In my Father's house are many rooms; if it were not so, I would have told you. I am going there to prepare a place for you. And if I go and prepare a place for you, I will come back and take you to be with me that you also may be where I am. (John 14:1-3)

The apostle Paul had a difficult time deciding whether he wanted to live or die. He wrote, "For to me, to live is Christ and to die is gain" (Philippians 1:21). He explained his dilemma in the following verses. When we die, we will be with Jesus Christ, "which is better by far." Heaven will be better than we can imagine, for "No eye has seen, no ear has heard, no mind has conceived what God has prepared for those who love him" (1Corinthians 2:9). Knowing the wonderful and eternal future that awaits us gives us hope and courage to endure our trials.

Think of all the risk takers who trusted the Lord. Abraham (sacrificing Isaac), Rahab (saving the spies), David (a shepherd boy facing the giant Goliath), Elijah (challenging Baal's prophets), Esther (approaching the king without being summoned), Daniel's friends (and the fiery furnace), Peter and Paul (preaching the gospel in hostile environments), and the list goes on. Who else from the Bible took deadly risks?

_____

Prayer combined with trust is fundamentally involved in these risk takers' lives. "The righteous man is rescued from trouble and it comes on the wicked instead" (Proverbs 11:8). The account of Esther, Mordecai, and Haman is a great illustration of that verse! The men who accused Daniel and had him thrown to the lions, and the men who threw Shadrach, Meshach, and Abednego into the furnace also received what was intended for God's faithful. Can you think of any modern day risk takers who serve the Lord? _____

Any missionary comes to my mind. What risks, small or large, do you face in your life today?

_____

We risk our employment being Christians in the secular arena, we take risks when we tithe, and we risk friendships by sharing our faith. Americans have lost their jobs and businesses for adhering to God's design of marriage or for praying openly. Whenever we take a risk to obey the Lord, we have to trust Him. It's easy to say we trust God, but sometimes hard to do.

Have you ever taken a risk that involved exercising your faith? _____

Our biblical heroes of faith risked their lives to be obedient to God and serve Him. Can you do the same if confronted today? _____ Too many countries are intolerant to Christianity, and too many believers live with extreme oppression and persecution. How strong is your faith? You will learn the answer when you are tested. Trusting God is necessary to remain faithful.

When you do not understand your difficulties or are living with pain, injustice or religious persecution, pray to God, and trust Him for everything in this life and in the life to come. He is worth the risk because you win either way.

Prayer For Today:

Thank God that He has prepared a place for you to live with Him forever.

Ask God to help you be faithful in prayer – praying sincerely, humbly, expectantly, continually, and for others, so your trust in Him grows.

_____

_____

_____

Day Five: Benefits of Trusting God

I like the church sign that says, "The death benefits of the Christian are out of this world!" And yet, believers who trust God also receive benefits while still living on planet Earth. However, whoever disbelieves God's power and rule over everything cannot wholeheartedly trust Him. Anyone who secretly doubts His wisdom, goodness, and love will experience more hesitation and procrastination than service.

The Lord addressed those who sit on the fence — who acknowledge Jesus' identity, but never committed themselves to obey or serve Him. He called them "lukewarm Christians" and gave some warnings to them. In Revelation 3:14-16, He declared:

> These are the words of the Amen, the faithful and true witness, the ruler
> of God's creation. I know your deeds, that you are neither cold nor hot.
> I wish you were either one or the other! So, because you are lukewarm –
> neither hot nor cold – I am about to spit you out of my mouth.

James also addressed those who believe in the Lord, but do not act on their beliefs. He wrote that if a man claims to have faith but has no deeds, it is not a saving faith. In fact, faith by itself, if it is not accompanied by action, is dead.[64] Our faith must be evidenced with obedience. James warned that even the demons believe in God, and they shudder. But demons have rejected God's preeminence and instead serve Satan.

There is a difference between belief and faith. Belief is an intellectual assent, an agreement with a set of teachings. Faith produces a motivation to act on the belief, accompanied by a commitment of service. Saving faith transforms our conduct as well as our thoughts; a desire to love and please God materializes into obedience and coincides with trust. Therefore, if we cannot trust God, we have to question our faith. Trusting God means believing:

- He knows what is best for us
- He is in complete control
- He loves us and wants to give us what is best

- He is aware of all things
- He is able to provide for us
- He has absolute power

> "Do not be anxious about anything, but in everything, by prayer and petition, with thanksgiving, present your requests to God."
> Philippians 4:6

If we believe these truths, we can confidently obey the Lord and put our hope in Him. We often approach God when we encounter emergencies or big issues, but not for our everyday activities. Yet, God is Lord of our lives 24/7, no matter where we are or what we do. We can't compartmentalize Him or put Him in a box to open at church. Do we allow Him to be Lord over every part of our lives? Have we surrendered our ways for His way? When we truly trust God, we can wholeheartedly submit to Him. That means following His principles in the Bible for our daily living.

When we sincerely and completely trust God to provide for us, we will trust Him more than our bank accounts. We will pay our taxes, tithe, and give generously to those in need. God told His people to test Him in that area to see if He won't "throw open the floodgates of heaven and pour out so much blessing" when we give back to Him (Malachi 3:10).

If we trust God to help us serve Him, we will depend on Him (and not ourselves) for wisdom, strength, and the ability to carry out what He calls us to do. An advantage of trusting God is to be able to confidently put our feet in the water before we see God's provisions. (The priests, carrying the ark, had to enter the Jordan River before God separated the waters for them to walk through.[65]) The Lord acknowledges those who trust and obey Him, and rewards them for their faith.

Trusting God, coupled with prayer, reduces our stress level no matter what problems we may experience. Read Philippians 4:6 in the inset. What did Paul tell us to do instead of worry?

Believers who wholeheartedly trust God will make Him Lord over their lives and obey Him. What are some of their rewards and benefits?

Psalm 32:10 _____

Psalm 94:19 _____

Proverbs 3:6 _____

Isaiah 66:13 _____

Matthew 6:25,33 _____

John 5:24 _____

Philippians 4:7 _____

God's peace is different from the world's peace. His supernatural peace transcends all understanding. It doesn't come from positive thinking, good feelings, or an absence of conflict, but from believing God is in control. It is a deep-seated, confident assurance of His sovereignty at all times. This inner peace keeps us from anxiety and worry. What did Jesus say in John 14:27?

"_____ I leave with you; _____ peace I

_____ you. I do _____ give to you as the

_____ gives. Do not let your _____ be

_____..."

> *Giving our problems to God and trusting Him to do things in His way and in His time is the only way we can have true and lasting peace.*

Giving our problems to God and trusting Him to do things in His way and in His time is the only way we can have true and lasting peace. It is actually a relief to realize that God knows what is going on and is in total control. When we are in the middle of some problem and receive God's peace, it is confirmation that our sovereign Lord is working on our behalf. And we are awed when we see how He worked it out for our good. When we have this peace that only comes from God, we no longer fear the present or the future.

I am reminded of a movie where the act of kissing a person was taught as leaning in toward the person 90% and allow the other individual to come the last 10% of the way. Well, God has leaned in more than 90% of the way, making it easy for us to come to Him and rely on Him. When we choose to draw closer to God and trust Him with our lives, we experience things that are amazing. What does Ephesians 3:20 reveal?

"Now to him who is _____ to do _____

more than all we _____ or _____,

according to his _____ that is at _____

_____ us..."

Jesus Christ's power at work within us refers to the Holy Spirit, who supplies us with love, joy, peace, comfort, and direction. Read Romans 15:13. What does our God of hope fill us with when we trust in Him? _____

Think about what it means to have joy and peace. That is the life God intended us to experience when He created us for a relationship with Him. That is what faithful followers have waiting for them when they love, trust, and obey the Lord.

God loves you, cares for you, sees your troubles and tears, and reassures you that there is a purpose for each difficulty you experience. He is able to take every hardship and work it for your good because He is a good and powerful God. You can choose to be ruled by your feelings of anxiety, resentment, and grief, or you can choose to act on your spiritual beliefs and exercise your faith by trusting God. He is faithful and will not fail you. Life hurts, but not quite as much when you trust God through your troubles and tears.

When you become completely submissive to the Lord, you will receive His help and His rewards. You will love the abundant life He offers. Do you hear Him calling you? Your heavenly Father's arms are reaching out to you. He wants you to come to Him and receive His love. He wants your problems, cares and concerns, and all of your heart, soul, mind and strength. He wants you to experience Him and delight in Him in a way you never have before. Our Lord has so much He wants to give you. Submit all of your life and surrender your control to Him. Trust God wholeheartedly and the best part of your life will begin.

Prayer For Today:

Thank God for His love, wisdom, and power.

Ask God to take complete control of your life as you submit to Him and trust Him.

_____

_____

_____

For anyone who would like to submit, dedicate, or rededicate your life to God and who desire to trust Him wholeheartedly, just say a prayer like this:

My Father in heaven, I want to commit my life to You. I believe that Jesus Christ is God and that He died for my sins, arose from the dead, and ascended into heaven. I accept this free gift of salvation and ask You to forgive me because I know I have sinned against You and others. I need the Holy Spirit to work in me and to guide me. I want a deeper relationship with You, so enable me to submit myself totally to You. Help me to live for You and serve You. Continually remind me of Your power, wisdom and love for me. Teach me what I need to know and keep me from straying away from You. Father, since this life is short compared to our life after death, please make mine count for something good. Help me to trust You and prepare me for my eternal life with You. I pray this in the powerful name of Jesus, Amen.

Saying this prayer and sincerely meaning it will be the start of a new beginning. Whether you rededicated your life or gave it to God for the first time, He heard you and wants you to know how much He loves you. Keep talking and listening to the Lord – especially through reading the Bible. Since He is the author, His powerful words are on those pages. God's fingerprints - which are all over the Bible - make impressions on our lives. Let Him touch your heart, over and over again.

And now, "May the God of hope fill you with all joy and peace as you trust in him, so that you may overflow with hope by the power of the Holy Spirit" (Romans 15:13).

CHAPTER SIX DISCUSSION/REVIEW QUESTIONS

1. What do you fear the most? What needs to be accomplished in order to trust God with that fear?

2. How do you gain control of your emotions when they are running wild?

3. When was the last time you had a difficult time trusting God?

4. What reasons or excuses did you recently use to avoid serving God?

5. Share a time when you received more than you gave, (when serving God and others).

6. How often does your mind come up with Scripture when you need encouragement? Have you read enough of the Bible to know what God promises?

7. How hard is it for you to forgive someone who betrayed you? Someone who hurt your child or parent? Why do we have to forgive our enemies?

8. How do we go about making sure our prayers are in God's will?

9. Share how you were blessed by someone else serving the Lord. (How did their service benefit or encourage you?)

10. How much time do you spend praying for other people? What are the benefits from praying for others?

11. Why does God desire praise and thanksgiving in our prayers?

12. When have you been a recipient of answered prayers from others?

13. What risks do you take by being a Christian today?

14. Do you know anyone who is a lukewarm Christian? What can you do to help that person develop a deeper faith and more vibrant relationship with the Lord?

15. How does God reward us for obeying Him?

16. Can you trust God? Has your trust or faith increased after doing this Bible study?

Endnotes

1	Greek Strong's Number 4100	35	Psalm 34:3
2	Romans 10:9 footnote NIV	36	Jesus Loves Even Me – lyrics by Philip Bliss
3	Hebrew Strong's Number 982	37	John 21:20
4	Revelation 12:9	38	John 11:3
5	1 John 3:8	39	John 11:36
6	Revelation 12:10	40	1 John 3:18
7	Matthew 10:25	41	Colossians 3:12
8	Job 1:7	42	Hebrews 10:1-18
9	NIV Life Application Study Bible p. 13	43	Romans 9:5
10	Matthew 4:1-11	44	1 John 1:8; Romans 6:23
11	Luke 5:16	45	Mark 15:38
12	Exodus 33:7-11	46	Alfred B. Smith and Frances Townsend
13	Colossians 1:16-17 NIV Life Application Study Bible footnote	47	Romans 5:5
14	Genesis 3:14	48	Matthew 5:46
15	TLB 2 Corinthians 12:9	49	Acts 9:16
16	Hebrews 13:8	50	2 Corinthians 11:23-28
17	1 Samuel 8	51	Mark 14:33-34
18	2 Chronicles 20:15-17	52	Luke 14:27
19	Judges 7	53	Leviticus 11:45
20	Exodus 32:9-14	54	2 Thessalonians 2:13
21	Jonah 3:10	55	James 4:2
22	NIV Study Bible footnotes; Psalm 7:9	56	John 11:40
23	Psalm 139:16	57	Acts 4:13
24	Acts 15:8	58	Luke 9:1-2,6
25	NIV Study Bible dictionary	59	Psalm 17:3; Jeremiah 17:10; Revelation 2:23
26	Hebrew/Greek Key Study Bible by Zodhiates p. 1715	60	James 4:2
27	NIV Life Application Bible; Tyndale and Zondervan	61	Mark 14:60-61; Matthew 27:12-14
28	2 Chronicles 1:10-12	62	Luke 5:16
29	NIV Life Application Study Bible, page 840	63	Daniel 6:23
30	Job 1:1 footnote	64	James 2:14-26
31	Malachi 3:6; Hebrews 13:8	65	Joshua 3:13
32	Hebrew/Greek Key Study Bible		
33	John 12:28		
34	John 17:1		

Personal Notes

Personal Notes

Personal Notes

Personal Notes

Printed in the United States
By Bookmasters